MW01627035

Real Life. *Real Ladies.*

Short Stories from the Pew

Compiled by

Rita Klundt

Copyright @ 2021 Rita Klundt

All rights reserved. No part of this publication may be reproduced or transmitted in any form or by any electronic or mechanical means including photo copying, recording, or any information storage and retrieval system now known or to be invented, without permission in writing from the publisher or the author.

Scriptures marked NIV are from THE HOLY BIBLE, NEW INTERNATIONAL VERSION®, NIV® Copyright © 1973, 1978, 1984, 2011 by Biblica, Inc.™ Used by permission. All rights reserved worldwide.

Scripture quotation marked NLT are from Holy Bible, New Living Translation, copyright © 1996, 2004, 2015 by Tyndale House Foundation. Used by permission of Tyndale House Publishers, Inc., Carol Stream, Illinois 60188. All rights reserved.

Scriptures marked ESV are from ESV® Bible (The Holy Bible, English Standard Version®), copyright © 2001 by Crossway, a publishing ministry of Good News Publishers. Used by permission. All rights reserved.

Scriptures marked NASB are from New American Standard Bible
Copyright © 1960, 1971, 1977, 1995, 2020
by The Lockman Foundation, La Habra, Calif. All rights reserved.

Scripture quotations marked MSG are taken from THE MESSAGE, copyright © 1993, 2002, 2018 by Eugene H. Peterson. Used by permission of NavPress. All rights reserved. Represented by Tyndale House Publishers, Inc.

Scriptures marked NKJV taken from the New King James Version®. Copyright © 1982 by Thomas Nelson. Used by permission. All rights reserved.

Name: Compiled by Rita Klundt
Title: Real Life. Real Ladies: Short Stories from the Pew
ISBN: 978-1-952369-60-5
Subjects: 1. BIOGRAPHY & AUTOBIOGRAPHY/ Personal Memoirs
2. BIOGRAPHY & AUTOBIOGRAPHY / Women
3. BIOGRAPHY & AUTOBIOGRAPHY / Religious

Interior Design by Darryl Bennett
Cover Design by Robin Black
Cover Photo Credit: iStockphoto

Published by EA Books Publishing, a division of
Living Parables of Central Florida, Inc. a 501c3

EABooksPublishing.com

This book is dedicated to the church ladies who sat on the floor, read stories, and played with me when I was a preschooler; to the women who taught me in Sunday school, Girls in Action and Vacation Bible School; to my chaperones at church camp and on youth outings; to the pastors' wives who stepped out of their glass houses to be my friend; to the lovely ladies who provided beautiful harmonies whether they were in the church choir loft, in the fellowship hall, or in their homes; and to the ladies whose stories appear in this book for demonstrating true love, indescribable joy, unshakable peace, miraculous patience, genuine kindness, God's goodness, calm faithfulness, sacrificial gentleness and trustworthy self-control. Your lives are a beautiful chapter in God's story.

Table of Contents

Introduction *Rita Klundt* 9

Journey with Joyce *Cathy McAllister*.................. 13

A Special Day *Dawn Cook* 19

Commodities *Diana Parson* 23

The Sound of Hymnals *Rita Klundt* 29

On My Way Home
Stephanie Bridgeman-McClaskey 35

Healing for a Broken-Hearted Woman
Robin McClallen... 39

Remember Me? *Jan O'Bleness* 43

First Memory *Kathy Stanford* 47

Just Another Sunday *Jill McNicol* 49

Out of the Woods *Dawn Wright* 55

He Said Go. I Went. *Jenny Auxier*...................... 63

Stolen Joy *Rita Klundt*.. 67

A Thousand Second Chances *Sandra Taylor* 69

My Name is Marilyn *Marilyn Hurt* 77

Grandma and the Girdle *JoAnn Brown* 83

Through the Wringer *Natalie Schnoor*............... 85

I Like to Go to Church *Ellene Lisanby* 93

The Children's Home *Anita Allen* 99

For the Record *Anita Allen* 101

The Hardest Pain *Anita Allen* 103

Goodbye, Blue Hat *Aletha Oakley* 105

Love is Never Late *Kristi West Breeden* 107

His Strength. His Time. My People.
Dalene Stewart 111

An Encounter with God *Kathy Stanford* 121

The Fire *Lindsay Wineinger* 123

More than Two of Us
Holly Templeton Duckworth 131

Drive and Determination *Judy Mandrell* 135

When What You Want to Say
Won't. Come. Out. *Susan Walker*................ 141

Teach Me, Lord, to Wait *Jenny Auxier*............ 145

The New Teacher *Stacy Vickers* 151

My Return *P. J. Hill*.. 155

The Price of Caregiving *Rebecca Price* 161

As Rita listens to the stories of women across Illinois, she traces the hand of God in the details of each account. Rita knows the impact storytelling can have on a person, opening their mind to hope and the discovery of new possibilities. We all have a story connected to God's story. By retelling the story of others, Rita connects thoughts in such a way that others begin to look for God in their own experiences, ultimately pointing them to Jesus. I'm grateful for the stories God is writing across Illinois, and I'm grateful to Rita for telling those stories to a larger audience.

Carmen Halsey
Director of Leadership Development, Leadership Development Team
Illinois Baptist State Association

Introduction

I love a good story. Always have.

Some of my fondest childhood memories are of Mom reading to us. She knew how to voice a story off its pages, and I can't recall her ever stumbling over new or long words. Fairytales, nursery rhymes, the classics, and stories from her Bible all rotated into our nightly routine. When Sunday nights or Wednesday nights at church went long, and Mom was too tired for reading aloud, I pouted.

Mom had a way of selecting stories pertinent to the events of our day. I knew when she read the story of *Pinocchio* two nights in a row, it was for my benefit. Her purse-lipped smile with raised eyebrows told me so. All of her children were on the same sofa when she turned the book so we could see the illustrations, especially the size of Pinocchio's nose, but she held the page closer to me than to any of my three siblings.

Except to leave out the rare and unessential "naughty" word, Mom never dumbed down a book for her audience of four. She taught us important life lessons from between the lines in stories such as *Uncle Tom's Cabin* or *Little Women.*

The ten-year difference between my older sister and my baby brother didn't bother her—if the story was good. Mom could turn almost any book into a one-story-fits-all. She alternated between thick chapter books that might have no pictures at all, and those thin Little Golden Books with an illustration on at least every other page.

When my second-grade teacher ruined a good story by stuttering her way through a paragraph of simple words, I interrupted with, "My mommy is better at reading out loud than any school teacher."

The teacher's snappy suggestion that my mother come to school and read the next chapter caused me to cry in front of all my classmates. I still don't care for sarcasm. My blood pressure rises and I might just cry if I hear an adult stooping to use hurtful sarcasm against a small child.

Bedtime at our house could be delayed if Mom wanted to finish a chapter, yet the final kind of low-pitched sound that a book makes when you close it fast and hard on a good cliffhanger seemed to bring her delight. Maybe she planned it, or maybe that's just the way the pages turned.

I remember lying in bed, listening for her footsteps, and thinking. How mean and selfish of my mother to leave her four children wondering if a beloved heroine had only been horribly injured, or was already dead. When mom's steps took her back into the living room, I imagined her, with book open, satisfying her own curiosity. I accused her. She neither admitted guilt nor denied it, and I couldn't prove anything. Her bookmark, each time, was exactly at the cliffhanger.

So, that's how my love of story began.

Story time gradually transitioned from surrounding Mom on the sofa, getting close so all of us could see the pages, to watching most of our stories come out of a box on the other side of the room. It started with programs like *The Lawrence Welk Show* and *Gunsmoke*. Dad scrutinized what we watched and was quick to have us "turn off that box," but he joined us on Saturday nights.

Mom was the last of us to accept her stories via television. She would read, or sew, while the rest of us watched TV. Television in the sixties provided only three choices: ABC, NBC and CBS. Mom however, could choose from all sorts of books. If it wasn't already on our bookshelf, with a short trip to the library she could bring home a week's worth of great reading.

Conflict among any of us would be set aside to hear Mom read. While Mom was reading to us, every fight or harsh word spoken earlier in the day would be forgotten, and sometimes forgiven. Not so with made-for-television stories. Commercial announcements created opportunity for passing insults and punches. Playful hitting, kicking, and generally aggravating the person closest to us often escalated from tattling and sulking to dangerous sibling combat.

Television, with all its visual effects and emotion-stirring background music, competed with my mother's voice and oftentimes won. But stories told through "that box" don't lend themselves to pausing and enjoying well-crafted dialogue or contemplating a fast-moving and complex plot. Recorded stories allow for a rewind, but flipping back to a previous page is much easier.

My favorite form of storytelling is the oldest.

In the sixth chapter of Deuteronomy, Moses instructed a generation of Israelite people who hadn't experienced a life of slavery in Egypt or seen all the signs and wonders God did in the presence of their parents. He told them to pass on their family stories, to tell their children what God had done for them, and to teach them the Lord's commands. Where would we be without those stories?

I go to my family's reunions because they're on my calendar. Once I get there, I enjoy the meal; but I linger to reconnect with aunts, uncles, and cousins…and for the storytelling. Some of the best stories are told at dinner tables, on front porches, and over backyard fences. Anywhere two or more are gathered, there's potential for a great story.

Stories educate. They warn. They equip and inform. I've been inspired and empowered through the stories of ordinary, unlikely people. If a story can make me laugh or cry, I am changed. Benjamin Franklin knew the value of story. He is credited with saying, "Either write something worth reading or do something worth writing."

About 75 percent of the Bible is story. Maybe that's for people like me. Stories are a gift and part of God's grand design. That's true, even of fiction, or as Mom called it, "make-believe." If a story merely calls me to come rest my busy mind and sit for a while, that's a good thing.

Not long ago, I was carrying a box filled with heavy, but fragile, dishes up from our basement. I had some distance to go before setting it down. My arms ached. My fingers cramped enough that I feared losing my grip. A muscle in the area of my right shoulder and back burned as though begging for medical attention. But my cargo was precious. Dropping the box would be costly in both a financial and emotional way. If even one dish broke, I would grieve. Then, an opportunity to shift the weight from one arm and shoulder presented itself. My fingers could flex and get their color back. Halfway up the staircase, I took that opportunity.

No, my burden had not been fully lifted. Yes, the box was still heavy and awkward, but after a moment to readjust the load and consider what was ahead, I kept climbing. The pretty dishes made it, damage free, from that cardboard box in the basement to the lighted, glass box they now call home.

The short and true stories that follow have lightened my load. The women who gifted them to me are some of my favorite, Jesus-following, church-lady friends. They now offer a chapter of their lives to you. Be blessed.

–Rita Klundt

Journey with Joyce

April 25, 2005

We lived less than a mile apart, on the same street. So to have Joyce pull into our driveway and interrupt my yard work wouldn't have been unusual or alarming, except that we had been waiting a couple of weeks for her biopsy result.

"I have cancer. I'm gonna lose my hair. It's a rare form of cancer, and that's why it took so long to diagnose," she said. "He asked which oncologist I preferred, and the appointment is already made. We will decide on a treatment at that visit."

We stood in my driveway and cried. I was still in shock when Joyce backed into the street and headed toward home to make phone calls. She had given me permission to share her news with my family. My family was hers and hers was mine.

"Go ahead," she said through a smirk. "I'll be bald soon and everyone will know."

I remember praying for a miracle, but mostly telling God what I couldn't do, what I couldn't face and what I couldn't endure. Joyce and I were more than best friends and confidants. We were partners in a small business.

The next day she called and said, "Hey, are we painting today?"

"No. We just found out you have cancer yesterday."

"Cathy, it's not over till the Lord says it's over! We go on, just like before."

Our business was painting and selling molded plaster and glass, so we painted and made plans for our next craft show.

Over the next few weeks, I found it nearly impossible to focus on anyone but me. I loved Joyce, and if I could have, I would have cured her of the cancer. My thoughts and prayers however, were an awful lot about me. Three weeks in, I discovered that I was making a malignant tumor in someone else's body all about me—not a nice thing. I'm grateful for that early discovery, because Joyce had only twenty months more.

I was invited to go along with her and her family to the doctor. They were very gracious to me. The oncologist explained why the cancer was inoperable. The tumor was in the center of her liver and had invaded the bile ducts. Treatments would be three weeks on and one week off.

The morning of her first treatment I said, "Don't you want me to go with you?"

"No. I need to do this one by myself, but I'll call you when I'm done, and we can go for lunch."

It was still about me. *What do I say? What do I ask? What should we eat? What if she won't let me pay? Maybe I should make her some soup and insist she go straight home to rest.*

Joyce shared that the most difficult part of her first treatment was sitting in the cancer center, watching other patients and wondering about their lives and their cancers. She spoke many times of her acquaintances from the cancer center. I saw in Joyce that it wasn't even all about Joyce.

A faith-based cancer support group was started in the fall after her diagnosis. God had already prepared the heart of another friend and cancer survivor as she ministered to cancer patients by visiting them, praying with them, and offering help and encouragement. That year, Faith Force Cancer Support, a ministry for cancer survivors and their loved ones, was officially born.

Joyce and her husband were at the first meeting. I went along. She was the first of us to learn our motto scripture. I say "learn" because she memorized the words, but she also understood and lived out their meaning.

"Therefore we do not lose heart. Though outwardly we are wasting away, yet inwardly we are being renewed day by day. For our light and momentary troubles are achieving for us an eternal glory that far outweighs them all. So we fix our eyes not on what is seen, but on what is unseen, since what is seen is temporary, but what is unseen is eternal" (2 Corinthians 4:16–18, NIV).

Joyce always had a story to share with the group. Often, it was about her ongoing struggle with their insurance company. Who would've known that a person can walk into a cancer support meeting, where the topic of insurance is discussed, and walk out feeling hope? I'd never say it was easy, but there were many sweet times during those hard to hold meetings.

Other memories are a treasure. One day, in the middle of preparing for our church's Vacation Bible School, Joyce announced that she was tired.

"I have to lay down."

She stopped what she was doing and marched over to my couch. She napped while I did housework. I think we both needed a break from the repetitive cutting and pasting. I don't recall if she slept more than an hour, or less, but she sat up suddenly, happy and hungry.

"I need something to eat!"

This was about three weeks into her chemo treatments and the moment I realized what a roller coaster, both physically and emotionally, a battle with cancer could be. I can't explain how I felt that day as I prepared a snack for us, but Joyce had the energy to talk, and she allowed me to listen to her heart. I knew I was being blessed.

From the beginning, I felt helpless. I didn't know how to pray, what to say or do, or how to help her. She asked me, "How are you doing with all of this?"

"Not so good."

"Well, you're doing better than I would, if you were the one with cancer."

I had no idea what it was, but I must've been doing something right. I began pleading that day, "Lord, help me focus on my role as a best friend."

Joyce was praying too. For her to accept offers of help with housework and other chores, she had to be. I sensed her effort to help me, prepare me, and give to me.

"Wow! You really clean fast," she said. "Thanks. I almost wish I could do that myself."

I went home that day humbled and thankful to have anything to offer Joyce. Soon after, she began a new type of treatment that disturbed her liver and caused her abdomen to swell. The way I understand it, tiny radioactive pellets (or seeds) were shot into her liver.

"I don't mind the treatments," she said, "but I can't even bend over to put lotion on my feet or legs."

"I can get my pedicure tub and give you a little tender loving care?"

"Please. That would be great."

She relaxed, closed her eyes and took deep breaths. I still thank the Lord for that privilege, and Joyce appreciated it so much. I was both honored and humbled that day.

During one of her stays in the hospital, she expressed anxiety.

"I have a male nurse tonight. I'm not really comfortable with him."

This was not the first male nurse she'd had, but I figured she had her reasons. The next morning, I found her sitting up in bed.

"I had the best night! The nurse told me it was time for a bath. I thought to myself, *How is this going to happen? I can't get out of this bed.* Then he filled a basin, put it on the bedside table and told me to turn on my light when I was finished. I got the best backrub when he came back, and then he washed my hair. He used a bedpan. Can you believe it?" She added, "A clean one. It was the coolest thing. The curve fit my neck just right, and it felt so good. I didn't need to ask for a sleeping pill."

After that, I heard about her visit with the Lord.

"I was talking to Jesus," she said. "We talked for quite a while. I asked him to forgive me for not inviting you to sit and rest. Cathy, he showed me the most beautiful light show I've ever seen!"

I began to consider the medications they had given her. My thoughts returned to the night we brought her into the hospital and the look on the nurse's face as she parked the crash cart outside Joyce's room. Now, she's telling me about this light show and insisting her "Shepherd" had been the one showing it to her.

She warned me that some people would think it was medication.

"But Cathy, it wasn't any medication."

And I knew she was telling the truth. I always left Joyce's room with some measure of gratitude. That morning, I was grateful the Lord was comforting her, and me too.

By December of 2006, she rarely had a good day. That was the month of our last craft show together. She wanted and tried to get up and go every day, but her days were difficult, and her husband reported her nights to be restless.

"Cathy," she said one day, "You need Betty to help you get through this. And Venita."

Venita, together with her husband, had been the friend with the vision and passion to start Faith Force. Betty had been a faithful friend of ours for several years.

I didn't want to talk about it. Joyce wasn't "like a sister." She *was* my sister. Betty and Venita were good friends and "sisters in Christ," but one can't simply replace one sister with another, or even two. I couldn't talk about it.

It had been during one of Joyce's earlier hospital stays that Venita asked me if I'd like to be prayer partners. She gave me a folder with a list of concerns that cancer patients often have: things like fear and pain, family support and finances, death and the afterlife, effective treatments, dealing with chemo side effects, body image and the dreaded loss of hair. Everything on the list was common to most cancer patients, but I made them specific to Joyce when I prayed. Venita and I prayed daily, and in between, for several weeks. Neither of us mentioned the folder or our prayer list to Joyce.

When she saw it on my table one day, Joyce asked, "What's this?"

I shared with her as she wept. Joyce never did lose her hair. I was humbled.

The support group meetings in the weeks after Joyce died were different from the ones before. Difficult, but I learned about the kind of strength and peace that comes only from the Lord. Cancer survivors, caregivers and those who had lost loved ones all provided me comfort. The personal connections I made through Faith Force Cancer Support are precious to me. I still go to meetings. Everyone's experience is different. Each member, whether listening, or sharing concerns and helpful information, has something unique to offer.

Joyce didn't want pity, and like many cancer patients, she resisted help until she was helpless. When she accepted my offer to clean her house and that amateur pedicure, I think she knew it pleased our heavenly Father. She can't have known how much it comforted and lifted me.

So many funny stories to tell. I miss the fun. I miss my friend. I learned so much on my journey with Joyce.

"So encourage each other to build each other up just as you are already doing" (I Thessalonians 5:11, NLT).

–Cathy McAllister

A Special Day

My daughter, Emily, considers November 19 a special day. In 2007 she was only seven. That morning, I knew something was wrong so I took her to the doctor. My concern wasn't based on a typical reason one takes a child to the doctor. I couldn't pinpoint her symptoms or adequately defend my fears. Emily looked to be a beautiful picture of health.

"But something has been off," I repeated.

I sensed the doctor labeling me as crazy, or at the least, a waste of her time, but she did agree to run some blood tests. The lab results weren't available when I called the doctor's office first thing after lunch. The person answering the phone educated me about the meaning of the word "afternoon." She repeated what the doctor had said, "We'll let you know." I sensed I'd been a pest.

Twenty minutes later, a nurse called and asked where Emily was.

"She's at school," I said.

"You need to pick her up immediately and take her to the emergency room."

Using extraordinary calm, I asked, "Why? What's wrong?"

"Her glucose came back 864. Her blood sugar. It's 864." The nurse verified that I understood it was the emergency room connected to the children's hospital, and not the closest emergency room. I left work right away, collected my daughter from school, and then drove to the emergency room. Our recollections of that drive are somewhat different, both of them entirely accurate in our own minds.

Once in the ER, Emily was hooked up to monitors and other machines that have some sort of purpose. I quit counting the number of people who were buzzing around her bed. I moved from my chair in the corner to stand next to her until I was in the next doctor, nurse or technician's pathway. Moms who've been where I was that day understand that useless and helpless feeling.

"How long has she been diabetic?" a doctor asked.

"What?" I replied. "She's not a diabetic."

Everyone's attention turned to me. I'm not sure if their faces expressed pity or shock that I didn't know my own child was diabetic. A new level of fear wanted me to panic. Something had been "off," and that something could not be cured with an antibiotic or any other pill. I was scared. Seven-year-old Emily was scared.

Two tests had already confirmed a diagnosis of Type 1 diabetes. The third test result came back that same day. It supported what the doctors already knew.

Before she was settled into a regular hospital room, Emily knew more about Type 1 diabetes than most adults. The two of us had a lot more to learn over the next few days. Medical terms and serious consequences (if we made a mistake) terrified me, but I worked to not let my anxiety show.

I cried quietly while she slept, or I escaped to a hallway if tears threatened while she was awake. There was nothing we could have done to prevent this lifelong fight, and we couldn't delay it. Facing it was our only option. I worried that Emily might be a better actor than me.

I prayed, not with churchy words or even complete sentences, but silently between breaths and words. God didn't answer me in the way I wanted or expected. He gave me what I needed.

Adults, I hear, are often overwhelmed by the instruction and practice with the equipment used to manage diabetes. My Emily, who had yet to learn long division, could recite patient precautions and demonstrate her competence with needles. I remember the events of that hospitalization well. I never will forget how God watched over us or how he answered the prayers for my little girl.

Emily looked up to me from her vantage point of a hospital bed and said, "At least I'm not allergic to peanut butter."

Yes, the everyday struggles that come with managing Type 1 diabetes mean there are "off" days for Emily, which means there have been a lot of "off" days for me too. Yes, every day, we pray for a cure. But November 19 is special. Our family may be the only one to recognize and celebrate “I’m not allergic to peanut butter” day.

–Dawn Cook

Commodities

Grey gravel and dust churned below the rusted-out floor of the truck. It hadn't rained all summer, and dust was everywhere. Dad had put a metal tray over the hole, but when he cleaned out the truck last week, he forgot to put the tray back on the floor. I watched in fascination and then announced that I thought I could fit my foot in the space.

Dad didn't yell often, but he did now. "Keep your feet outta that hole! You wanna lose your legs?"

I wasn't sure that would happen, but not wanting to take a chance, I pulled my feet up on the worn seat. Tape covered the bigger crack, while smaller lines spider-webbed out from under the tape.

The last time Dad had taken me for a ride in the truck, we found a dog. It was running loose, no collar. Dad stopped at the nearest farm and inquired about the dog. The farmer said it was dumped, and Dad said he would take it home. That dog was a good dog. I loved riding home with that big old dog leaning on me, and his tongue hanging out. We named him Scraps.

This time, I didn't think the ride would be as good. Dad held on to the steering wheel with clenched hands, and he yelled about the hole. And he didn't talk. Usually we told jokes and sang songs. This time … silence. All I knew is that we were going to town, and I didn't think we would come home with a dog.

Just outside of town, Dad pulled over at a little park. He turned off the engine and just looked at me. I suddenly had a scared feeling. I remembered that he and Mama were arguing. Were they getting a divorce? Was this what the drive was all about?

Dad sighed.

"Sis," he said. My name wasn't Sis; it was Diana. But Dad often called me Sis, especially when he had a job for me to do, like bringing up the cows from the pasture by myself.

"Sis, I need to talk to you about something."

Uh oh. Here it comes. This would be when he said that he and Mama were getting a divorce. I wasn't quite sure what divorce meant. Paula, who was in my grade, just went away when school was over a couple years ago. She was gone all summer, and when she got back, I asked her where she was.

"I went to my dad's," she informed me.

Her dad's? Her dad's what?

"My parents got divorced," she explained, and she looked sad. "My dad lives over in Shelby now."

I still didn't understand, but I knew that whatever it was, it was bad.

"Sis? Do you like butter?"

Butter? What did that have to do with divorce?

"You and Mama are getting divorced!" I blurted and started to cry. I couldn't help it. The tears just got huge and rolled out. I dug out a hanky from my pocket and tried to wipe the stream. Dad got out his big red hanky and handed it to me.

"Blow your nose," said Dad. I snuffled and blew and wiped my eyes again.

"It's been a tough year," Dad continued.

"You're going to move away and I can only see you at summer, and—and—and I don't want this!"

Dad's mouth had a tiny smile at the edges. I thought that was strange, but it didn't last long.

"No, Diana. I'm not moving away. We are not getting divorced. I just wanted to talk with you about, well, about how hard life is right now."

I knew we were poor, sort of. I mean, we had a house and clothes and stuff. And we had lots of fun playing games and running around the farm and riding bikes and building the tree house out of that junk wood in the shed, and singing silly songs at night. But I knew Mama and Dad argued, and it was about money. And I knew that our old truck didn't look too great. And I knew that when I needed a dime to go to the pay assembly at school, Mama told me that she didn't have any dimes, and then her face got all red.

I took a deep breath. "How tough?" I didn't even really know what that meant.

"I don't want you to worry none. But we have to save money."

I nodded. I understood that, especially after the dime business.

"We don't want you kids to ever be hungry. So they have this thing in town now where we can go, and they will give us boxes of food. For free. You like butter?"

I nodded.

"Well, these boxes have butter, real butter in them. No oleo. And peanut butter. And molasses. You can mix the butter and molasses, and spread it on bread, real good. All sorts of food. Sound good?"

I could only nod again.

"Here's the deal, Sis. Your mom doesn't want these boxes of food. It kind of scares her. And I need you to help her know that it's good food and that you like it. Think you can do that?"

Another nod. Dad raised one thumb. I raised a thumb and we touched thumbs. It was our promise with no words. I was silent as we drove on in to town and found the brick building with the food boxes. So no divorce. That was good. And food boxes with real butter. That sounded good. But talking to Mama if she was sad and scared and mad, not good.

We loaded the boxes and headed home. The lady gave me an extra empty box that I put on the floor of the truck, and put my feet into it.

I was amazed at how much stuff the lady put in the boxes: oatmeal, cornmeal, some kind of meat in tin cans, potatoes and onions and carrots, olives. YES! Olives! Mama and Dad never bought olives because Mama said they were too expensive. I loved, loved, loved olives. And here was a big old tin can full of olives!!! And there was peanut butter and butter and beans and peas and rice and a huge block of cheese. Dad said it was real cheese, not that Velveeta stuff. And there was milk, but it was a powder.

There was so much that it took six boxes to carry it all. The lady said that was the right amount for a family of six for a month. She gave me a book with recipes to use the food, and I read it on the way home. The book said it was "commodity" food, but I thought it was ordinary food, except it was all in big tin cans.

The book had a recipe for Spanish rice. I had studied about Spain, and it was so glamorous with fans and black lace and bulls running in the streets.

"I'm going to make this Spanish rice when we get home," I announced.

"What's it got in it?"

"Un, rice and tomatoes and peppers and spices and stuff. And hamburger."

"I think there were cans of tomato juice in the boxes," said Dad. "No peppers that I recall, and no hamburger. But hey, there's the meat in the tins; can you use that?"

"Sure!" I had no idea what kind of meat it was, but I was willing to try.

"Good. Talk to your mom about it. Tell her you want to try to cook this."

When we arrived home, the other kids came out and helped carry in the boxes. Scraps was wagging his tail and getting in the way. Mama was not in the kitchen, and didn't come in until Dad left to put the truck away. We excitedly showed her all the good food. She just stared at it—lips tight—shaking her head. She had little tears in her eyes.

"Look, Mama! Butter! Real butter! And Mama! Olives! And I have this book and it tells how to make Spanish rice and I want to try to make this for supper. Can I please? Will you help me?"

She got out a big skillet and I put butter into it. Then the rice. Mama said to keep stirring it until it got brown. Then we opened the tomato juice and poured over the rice. I chopped up an onion to add. The meat in the tin was sort of like ham, but you could tell it was in pieces and pressed back together. I looked at Mama with questions and she just nodded. I dumped in the meat.

It was smelling so good, and Dad just kept talking about how good it smelled and how he couldn't wait to taste it. Mama still didn't say anything. We sat down, and Dad prayed.

"Thank You, Father, for what we have." He paused.

"For what You have given us." Another pause.

"Please bless us and keep us. Amen."

The Spanish rice was good. I had wondered about the meat, but it was okay. We had olives to go with it. Dad asked me to make it again. Mama said nothing.

After supper we cleaned the kitchen and I started to put the dishes away.

"Mama? Did you like the Spanish rice?"

She nodded, and then said, "You did a good job on it."

"But Mama?" I stopped. I didn't know what to say.

She lifted her apron and wiped her eyes, and then drew me over to the table and we sat down.

"I'm sorry that I'm crying, Diana I really am. But this is government food. Commodities."

That word again. Commodities.

"Taking food from the government means that I can't feed you enough. And. And ..."

I waited. I knew the garden didn't have much this year, and the apple tree only had a few apples. Mama was usually canning food all summer, and now that I thought about it, she didn't can much at all this year.

"They publish in the paper the names of everyone who gets government food. I'm so embarrassed. I can't show my head at church or in town."

She cried openly. And I hugged her. I didn't know what else to do. I didn't want to starve. Not that I had ever been hungry. But starving sounded so awful. I knew Mama didn't want us to starve. She was always cooking and telling us to take seconds. But Dad didn't want us to be hungry, either. I just didn't know what to do.

"I don't want you to have a bad name," she sobbed. "I should be the one who feeds you. Your dad should never have taken that food!"

The little kids were all standing in the doorway to the living room, looking at us. I looked up and saw my dad standing in the doorway to the porch. He motioned to the little ones to come over, and he came over and wrapped his arms around all of us.

"It's going to be okay," he whispered. "It's just for a little while. Just until we get back on our feet again. I promise. This is how I have to take care of you right now."

Then he bent and kissed her. Usually when that happened, we kids just whooped and danced around and got kind of silly. But that night, we just stood in silence, watching our parents kiss in the kitchen.

Dad left to finish the evening chores, and the little ones went back into the living room.

Mama took a deep breath. "Let's make Spanish rice again someday," she said, and then she put the butter and cheese into the icebox and shut the door.

–Diana Parson

The Sound of Hymnals

My older sister, Janice, was not particularly fond of Mrs. Curtis and begrudged that we provided the old lady transportation on Sundays. The back seat of our car was crowded with an extra body occupying a window seat. The scent of Mrs. Curtis's cheap, dime store perfume rubbed off on the person sitting next to her. Janice made sure that was me.

Mrs. Curtis offered candy to both of us, but Janice always declined the little treats. She claimed not to like that kind of candy. After spending an unknown number of weeks, or months, in the deep, dark crevices of a big pocketbook, the hard sweets often required a significant investment of time separating a tacky, but edible, candy from the tiny shreds of wrapper that stubbornly remained. One small piece could collect an extraordinary amount of lint.

I could be tempted by things other than candy, and Mrs. Curtis knew it. We had created a Sunday morning ritual, cued by the music director stepping off the platform and the preacher heading toward the pulpit. The two would pause for a customary handshake.

The resonant sound of hymnals dropping randomly into their wooden pew racks lasted only long enough for me to lip-sync the words, "One-Mississippi, two-Mississippi, three-Mississippi." I supposed my juvenile method of measuring time was as accurate for a congregation of more than one thousand as it was for our congregation of fifty.

All the hymnals would not be returned to a rack. Mrs. Curtis always reserved two and placed them next to where she sat. She looked innocent enough, facing the front of the sanctuary, even religious, but her right hand rested on those hymnals calling me to nap time with an audible and rhythmic tapping of her fingers. I answered her call by scooting to her end of the pew and laying my head on those hymnals. Unable to dangle her arm in its natural state, with me so close to her side and in her space, she'd shift her weight, lift her elbow to the back of the pew and place her hand on my shoulder.

Four of those brown, well-used, soft-bound hymnals would have made a better headrest, but only two were within an arm's distance of Mrs. Curtis. I preferred a warm lap, but Mommy's had been handed down to my baby sister, and Mrs. Curtis… well, she was a very round woman. Her lap had been reduced to a pair of boney knees. A couple of hymnals had to do.

I can't say how old I was when our ritual began, but one of my earliest memories involves a particularly itchy sweater being placed over me. Except for the pleasure it gave my friend to care for me, I would have removed it. They say I was an adorable four-year-old. Some aging photos would support that, but on Sundays, Mrs. Curtis used the word "pretty." That, as much as anything, could be the reason I loved the woman.

I seemed to be the only one to appreciate her weekly reports that lasted from the time our car pulled away from the Golden Arms apartment complex until we stepped into the church building. A time or two, Daddy interrupted Mrs. Curtis mid-sentence, calling her stories "gossip."

My Daddy and big sister had their reasons—most of them valid, but I could be swayed by my sweet tooth and a couple of brown hymnals.

When I was four, almost five years old, Janice said, "Rita was snoring during the sermon."

I don't believe Janice meant to tattle, but I wished she'd started a different dinner conversation. Humorous banter bounced across the dinner table at my expense. Daddy changed the mood with an unexpected and non-debatable mandate.

"No more sleeping during church."

I wondered who would tell Mrs. Curtis, but was afraid to ask. Wondering turned to worry. Worry turned into spite. For the first time, I called my father "Dad" instead of Daddy. Mommy had the audacity to support his mandate. She too should feel some pain. I determined, from that day forward, to call her "Mom."

They must have felt some sort of sting at the sound of their new names and the loss of my affection, but neither of them let it show.

The next Sunday, I gave Mrs. Curtis a long gaze before I sat up straight and turned my eyes, but not my attention, toward the pulpit. She offered a sad, understanding nod before placing her hymnals in their rack. They would no longer be needed as sermon-time pillows. Mom got a gaze too, but she ignored me.

My friend Deloris, two pews in front of us, occupied her time with crayons and a coloring book. She was my age, but allowed to bring trinkets to church. Steve was my age. His family needed an entire pew. His dad seldom came to church, but the rest of the family, Grandma included, attended every Sunday. Grandma closed her eyes and sometimes snored during sermons. The kids talked out loud and made frequent trips to the restroom and drinking fountain. I'd seen Steve's homemade sling shot and was fairly certain it was one of his spit wads that landed in Deloris' hair. Someone should let her know, but it couldn't be me—until after church.

Janice carried a purse to church, but how much entertainment can a few tissues, a coin purse, and a ChapStick® provide? As an eight-year-old, she'd had more practice sitting up and being quiet.

With my eyelids heavy and my chin about to fall to my chest, I could sense one of Mom's eyes reminding me that sleep was forbidden. That's when the attack happened.

Just loud enough for her to hear me, I said, "Mom, I have ants in my pants."

She looked down, and leaned an ear toward me. Using my best church whisper, I repeated, "I have ants in my pants."

She heard me. Janice heard me and giggled, but mom gave me a tight-lipped smile and nothing more. My best attempt at sitting still and listening wasn't good enough. I tried again, but those ants!

"Mom. I really do have ants in my pants."

As much as I had perfected the "church whisper," Mom had learned to communicate a stern "No." She could breathe normally, tighten certain muscles in her face and provide explicit instruction, all without her making a sound. I could tell, by looking at my mother, if someone sang a sour note, if the sermon was going overtime, or if someone else's kids were misbehaving. I knew when her "No" was absolute.

I tried harder. I swung my legs, back and forth, then in coordinated circles. A stretch might work, but without that natural urge, it didn't. I used an elbow to brush against my baby sister. She pulled her leg away from me and did that "leave me alone" thing babies do, but she didn't wake or cry. I was miserable, and no one cared. I looked to Mrs. Curtis. She pretended not to notice me.

Weeks earlier, a conversation between mom and a couple of her church-lady friends had to do with having ants in your pants. These were the kind of ants that were attacking me now. I knew it. Like they had described, I was restless and aggravated by the feeling. Crazy was only moments away unless those ants would leave me alone. It was a horrible situation. This type of ant is not easily banished. Mom couldn't send them away with one of her looks. I doubted the preacher could pray them away. Now wouldn't be the time, and Mom wouldn't like it if I asked him for such a favor.

I tried listening to the preacher. I concentrated and willed those ants to leave, but they didn't. Nothing worked. Exaggerating my wiggle and squirm went without response. Any more drama, and I'd have unfavorable attention from Dad.

Then, a five-letter word changed everything. That single word holds phenomenal power. It would take decades, and a child of my own, before I'd fully realize the pull of one short word on a mother's heart. It passed through my manipulative little mind, and flowed through my soul in one moment of desperation. It prompted my mother to action.

"*Mommy*. I really do have ants in my pants."

A baby held to her chest with one hand and tugging on my elbow with the other, off we went to the ladies' room. Four black, patent leather shoes clicked on gray floor tile. She paused long enough to question me before we made it all the way to the restroom at the back of the sanctuary.

"What do you mean?" She jerked my elbow a little. "Ants in your pants!"

Based on the number of people who turned their heads, her church whisper was heard by half the congregation.

Still whispering, but red-faced, she announced. "You went pee-pee just before church started."

Mom watched as I bunched up my full skirt and started to pull down my panties. I realized she was expecting to see an army of ants. It was show time and the main characters in my drama had already left the stage. She made me sit for a few minutes. No results, and not one ant.

"They fell out when I stood up." And that is precisely what had happened.

I don't remember her saying anything, but I imagine that her lips were pressed together and not smiling as we slipped back into our usual pew.

The only repercussion from my little attack of restlessness was some teasing over the next few months. Janice found any and all my movements an opportunity to entertain.

"What's the matter, Rita? Got ants in your pants?"

Mom thought the story of *The Little Boy Who Cried Wolf* would teach me a lesson, so she read it to me several times over the next few weeks. She must not have known that listening to her read was my favorite form of entertainment. I thought it best to be a big girl and quietly accept the discipline.

To this day, I don't "cry wolf." I still have occasional attacks of "ants in my pants," and the sound of hymnals dropping into their racks makes me sleepy.

–Rita Klundt

On My Way Home

"A single moment of weakness is nothing to get too worked up about." That's what I told myself.

Usually, by this point in the weekend, I had spent all my money, not shown up for work, and wasn't sure if I still had a job. Details from the night before were sketchy, but my son would be home from his father's later in the day. I usually remembered that. I had to make myself look more like a human before he saw me.

I stayed in bed just a little while longer before crawling to the bathroom where I forced water down … just to throw it back up. I called it pumping my own stomach. A whole weekend without eating or drinking anything other than booze and drugs will make a person sick! Who knew? But that was my life.

Like a professional party-girl warrior, I ignored the familiar feeling of defeat, shook the fog from the night before, and faced this all too typical Sunday afternoon. A steamy shower dulled the stench of booze still seeping from my pores. I gave myself permission not to remember the past day and a half.

Blacking things out was a skill I had mastered long before I ever touched a drop of alcohol. Creating a convenient reality came even easier after a few drinks. All I had to do was apologize early and often for things I may or may not have done or said.

But had I really said those awful things to my dearest friend without the slightest bit of restraint or tiniest sting of regret? What does she remember? Who else had been on the receiving end of my lashing out? I would ask her to forgive me. She always did. I'm grateful for the fog, but tired of asking forgiveness for things I don't fully remember.

It's not easy to get yourself out of a situation after being rude and crude to your best friend, asking for the details of what you did and then begging forgiveness, not knowing what you did or what the consequences could be. By this time, I had reached the point of not wanting to know. *If I don't remember, don't tell me.* Without the memory, shame couldn't touch me.

Most people would probably leave the situation alone, or at least wait for the storm to settle before trying to patch things up. But not me. Partly because I needed a friend to help fix my life. Also, because I needed to manipulate—some would say obsess about a situation until I found a way to make myself the victim. Poor me! Poor me! Pour me another!

Of course, my friend didn't answer at the first ring or the first few of my text messages. I kept calling. She finally answered, only to yell at me, but for someone with abandonment issues, any response is better than no response. A hint of pity came through her voice, and I played on it.

"It's not my fault. I'm not that person. I drank too much. I don't remember."

She yelled some more.

I threw in the word "we," including her as my co-conspirator, but this was not our first dance. I repeated "I'm sorry" until she forgave me—again. She helped me make sense of a few things; even how situations in my childhood had trained me to make awful, self-destructive choices. Except this time, she finished the conversation and disappeared.

That downward spiral? It's not a silly cliché. It was my reality.

I reached out to my father (actually a foster parent). He always had answers, and had a history of fixing my big mistakes.

"I can't help you this time. Do you know what an enabler is?"

He didn't need to hear an answer, and I knew better than to beg. He suggested returning to church or some sort of counseling. I'd lost my job, my apartment, and was one or two incidents away from losing my son, whom I wholeheartedly believed would be better off without me. I considered suicide.

Learning that I had been pregnant had been enough motivation for me to stop the drinking and drugs … immediately. But now, my only reliable relationship came in a bottle, and my little boy had become the child I once was.

My birth parents, friends, and lovers had all abandoned me, and now my foster parents were detached and done with rescuing me. I saw no way out and prayer was all I had left. I hadn't the slightest idea what I was getting myself into and I didn't expect that God would answer.

I remember being six years old and praying that my mother would get arrested or go to rehab. At least then I would know she was alive and safe. Big prayers for a child so small. I envisioned my son having thoughts like that about me. Suicide was no longer an option.

I prayed.

Two days later, it was a Tuesday. I remember because I was waiting for my son to go to his dad's so I could go out. Often, I took him to the park behind my house, and when he was either tired from swinging and climbing, or I was bored, we'd walk to the church that backed up to the park. During the week, when no cars were in the parking lot, I'd sit on the steps and smoke while my son played on the handicap ramp.

On this particular day, after playing at the park, we walked to the church. I was enjoying my cigarette. He ran back and forth on the ramp several times before stopping at the top of the ramp to pull on the handle of the church's front door. For the first time ever, he opened it.

"Get away from there!" I yelled. "We need to go."

I put out my cigarette as a tall and leggy man stepped out the door.

"Hello," he said.

"Hi. We were just leaving."

He said something like we were fine, and then asked me if there was a church I attended.

I lied. "We're new to the area and haven't had a chance to find one yet. At least not one where we feel at home." I impressed myself with my ability to make someone think I was something I wasn't.

He told me about a dinner the next day and the Bible study that followed.

"We'd love for you to come. Every Wednesday at 5:30."

Surely he could see the hesitation on my face. Then he said something, as if he was reading my mind, "We're not a judgmental church; we are a family, all broken, trying to find our way together."

I can't go to church. I'm a mess … a real messy mess. But his words burned in my mind.

I didn't go out that night. Instead, I spent the evening alone, feeling sorry for myself and mulling over all the wrongs that had been done to me and by me. I battled with the idea of attending the church the next day, or not. Before I fell asleep, I decided, "What do I have to lose?"

The next day, I walked myself and my son to the church, feeling completely uncomfortable and out of my element, but Silas (that's my boy!) opened the huge door like a little super hero, and I stayed.

I didn't know it then, but my new life started that Wednesday evening.

–Stephanie Bridgeman-McClaskey

Healing for a Broken-Hearted Woman

If I'd really known how broken I was, I probably wouldn't have come. Only thinking that I may be able to help others in a similar situation to mine helped me join a post-abortion healing group. I thought I had settled it all with God a few years ago when I told Him I was sorry for taking the life of my child.

Unfortunately, instead of feeling better as time passed, I began to feel the ache of losing a child more deeply than ever. The ache had become a pain that felt as if a bowling ball had settled on my chest. The abortion, thirty-five years or so earlier, had left an indelible mark on my heart that unbeknownst to me affected nearly all of my relationships. My children had suffered having an emotionally distant mother, one who was so busy keeping her secret that sharing anything from the closed door of her heart just wasn't going to happen.

As a Christian, I hadn't been taught that abortion is wrong, but I knew, deep inside, that it was. I don't remember anyone ever talking to me about it. No sermon, no flyer in the church vestibule, no women's club meeting speaker or mention of abortion at home.

My mother took me to a doctor who suggested the option of abortion when I became pregnant at the age of nineteen, but at that time I chose to have my sweet girl, and although I was ignorant of how to either be married or raise a child, we struggled through getting to know each other as a little family.

The first pregnancy had brought destruction in the form of uterine tears and bleeding that required seventeen intrauterine injections to quell the flow (a fact no one bothered to tell me until I saw the hospital bill weeks later). The nurse happily explained that they had “almost lost me” on the operating room table.

Add a bit of poverty, being away from home for the first time in a new city, the emotional ups and downs and lack of sleep that comes with a colicky baby with a milk allergy, and maybe some hormone fluctuations too … let’s just say I was a mess.

Lo and behold, I become pregnant again. (Yes, I know about birth control, I was just a little inefficient with the application in my sleep deprived state.) I visited the county’s health department and the services of an abortion doctor were recommended. The nurse said there would be “a little pin-prick of pain” and then it would “all be over.” Not so. The emotional and spiritual consequences remained, even as the physical “problem” went away.

I came to know, years later, that my physical “problem” had been a boy. Some people say God doesn’t speak, but I know He does. He comforts, He corrects, He tells us that He loves us, and when we repent, He washes away our sin and He remembers it no more (Psalm 103:12 paraphrase). As far as the East is from the West, He removes the sting and stain of our sin.

I asked Him once about the effect the abortion had on my other two children, the one that came before the abortion, and the one that came after. What I was really asking was whether my sin had also brought destruction into their lives. Another layer of guilt that needed to be washed away. I believe that God, in His mercy, alleviated both the angst and the guilt of this newly discovered effect of the abortion when He assured me that He didn’t remember it. What an amazing feeling of freedom to know that such a terrible black mark on my soul was truly not being held against me. It had been washed away and I was clean.

With that knowledge, came the knowing that God, Himself was in charge of my children. Both the one in heaven with Him, and the two left here on earth. He had a plan for all of their lives, and was big enough to work it out for their good.

Freedom was waiting for me. But first, I needed to come out of hiding … out of my hurt and out of my shame. The process began when I shared my darkest secrets with the One who loves me without measure, and five women who understood my pain. My Heavenly Father directed me toward post-abortion healing classes, and now I’m praying He will guide other women as they seek His forgiveness and healing, that they may be able to look at their choice through the eyes of God's redeeming love and grace. He put me right back on track to fulfill the destiny He had planned for me before I was conceived.

He has a good plan for every broken woman's heart.

–Robin McClallen

Remember Me?

I was excited and scared, but ready my first day of junior high school. I had attended the same neighborhood grade school for six years and knew all fifteen of my classmates, the names of their siblings, and what their mothers looked like. They knew me, too. We were all excited to have earned a promotion to seventh grade. Junior high school! There would be a different teacher for every subject and classes more interesting than the basic reading, writing and arithmetic.

I woke early to my own alarm clock that September morning. Mom wouldn't have to wake me. I was practically a grown up. My mind was going in circles; there were so many things I had to check before leaving for school. The new outfit and shoes were where I'd put them the night before. That was easy. My hair was freshly cut and easy to style. So, I gathered my bag of school supplies and all my books on that crisp morning. A last-minute check that I had my class schedule, and the shiny new padlock for my locker wasn't necessary. I'd already checked them at least a dozen times. Oh, how I hoped I could remember where my locker was located and the combination.

Mom looked at me differently as she handed me lunch money. I wouldn't be coming home at lunchtime for a tuna or bologna sandwich. Surely, her look was because she would miss me. The extra nickel for an ice cream sandwich was our secret. My little sisters might get jealous if they knew.

Out the door, I started my eight-block journey to Washington Junior High School. My best friend met me on our usual corner and off we went, but in a new direction. The chattering about classes and teachers lasted for the seven and a half blocks of wider, busier streets. Then, we stepped onto the sidewalk surrounding our school.

There must be at least one hundred seventh graders here!

If I had known there were three times that many I might have turned and ran home.

Those were the biggest doors I'd ever seen. We looked at each other, took deep breaths and funneled through with the other students. My friend went her way, and I followed the numbered doors toward my first class, homeroom. We had been together six hours a day, five days a week, and nine months a year for six years. I was scared!

I was also shy and grateful that none of my friends could see the terror on my face.

My homeroom class was English, not much of a challenge for me. Dissecting sentences was easy, and I loved to read. This class, I expected, would be a breeze. The teacher, Mr. Wicks, was tall and slender. His big smile welcomed and charmed me right away. Black horn-rimmed glasses hinted of his personality and matched his teacher-like clothes. This was his first job out of college. We were his first official class. He had been a cheerleader and brought that enthusiasm with him by turning cartwheels every day as he entered the classroom. English was going to be fun!

I had always been a good student. My written assignments were completed on time and well done. I usually knew the answers when teachers called my name, but because I was shy, some degree of coercion was necessary for me to raise my hand or volunteer.

One of our first assignments for Mr. Wicks was to write what he called a "theme." I was proud of mine. Mom checked my grammar, spelling and punctuation, but found nothing to correct.

Then came the day when my row was to stand and read our themes in front of the class. My theme would be as good as any and better than most, but that wouldn't matter if my voice and knees wouldn't cooperate.

Oh no, it's my turn! Like the students before me, I stood at the side of my desk and started reading. Somewhere in my theme I used the word can't. No big deal, except I pronounced the word "caint."

Mr. Wicks interrupted my reading and asked, "How do you spell "caint?"

"C-A-N-apostrophe-T."

He called me to his desk. I was certain my classmates saw my red face and would be laughing soon. But when I reached the teacher's desk and raised my head, I saw they were looking down, pretending to focus on their books. Mr. Wicks instructed me to repeat "I can't say caint" until I got it right. I got it right after a couple of tries, but he made me repeat, "I can't say caint."

My mouth was dry, and the words were forced, but for what seemed about fifteen minutes, I repeated, "I can't say caint." Tears were dripping from my cheeks when, thank goodness, the bell rang. My classmates busied themselves with closing their books and shuffling papers. They didn't speak to each other or look toward me or Mr. Wicks as they exited the room.

I went to my desk and gathered my books, but Mr. Wicks wasn't finished. He called me back to his desk. *What now? I'll be late for my next class. I know how to say can't!*

It was just the two of us in the classroom, but his second-hour students would be arriving. Was it not enough for him to embarrass me in front of twenty students? Would adding twenty more witnesses to my humiliation make him happy?

"I'm sorry." Mr. Wicks apologized. "I'm very sorry," he repeated. He went on to explain that speaking proper English was important. "You'll be speaking much more in high school, college, and for future job interviews," he said. He told me that preparing for life had to start early, and he saw potential in me.

"Don't be afraid to speak up in class, especially my class."

Mr. Wicks wanted the best for me. He had made a mistake as a new teacher. Washington Junior High was huge for both of us. Because of him, I registered for the speech classes that most of my friends avoided. I'm still not thrilled about public speaking, but if I need to, I can.

When I'm visiting with family at a reunion or traveling through some states during winter, I enjoy the sweet and nostalgic sound of a southern drawl. But I never say "caint." I recall Mr. Wicks, with his charming smile, as one of my favorite teachers. Somehow, I think, he remembers me.

–Jan O'Bleness

First Memory

I've been told that memory recall often starts with a traumatic experience. One of my earliest memories is from when I was about two and a half years old and we lived in a small duplex in the suburbs of St. Louis, Missouri. My baby brother had just made his appearance when, a week later, we added a puppy to our family. She was barely weaned and quite small, so naturally we named her Tiny. Her favorite place to sleep was in my dad's shoe.

Dad was home, so it must have been a Saturday. The June sun streamed through the open door of our miniscule kitchen. My mother had been baking and, as was her custom, she left the oven door open to let it cool down. Just then, my new little brother began to cry. As she and my dad went to check on him, Mom warned me not to touch the oven because it was "very hot." This was not a new instruction, and I had been a compliant child, so there was no worry that I would disobey.

After Mom and Dad left the kitchen, I turned my attention to Tiny. While I squatted to enjoy the soft fur of my new puppy, I considered the open oven door. It was the perfect height to use as a petting table. So, with great care not to touch the hot door myself, I lifted Tiny and placed her there.

Her immediate and desperate yelps shocked me. It never crossed my young mind that what would hurt me would hurt my dog. In her effort to escape the pain, Tiny ran back into the oven where she began to yelp even louder. I remember feeling confused and distressed because I couldn't reach her without touching the hot oven.

Tiny's persistent yelping quickly brought my parents! She was rushed to the vet. Her burns were treated, and she recovered with no lasting harm. In fact, she lived fifteen more years as a beloved family pet.

Looking back on the trauma of that experience, I recognize it as more than my first recalled memory. It was also the day I began to see the world beyond myself. Not only did I learn that hot for me was also hot for others; I began to understand the broader scope of how my actions affect those around me. And Tiny, who showed no lasting ill will toward me, was the beginning of many more important life lessons.

–Kathy Stanford

Just Another Sunday

I have been a preschool Sunday school teacher for more than thirty years. During some of those years I lived with the belief that I would one day have a child of my own. But God had other plans and has given me the honor of teaching little ones, beginning at age three, and then watching those little ones have their own little ones for me to teach. I've told my grown-up students that one day I was going to write a book, and it would be a best seller because they would purchase all the copies to protect themselves from the stories I had to tell. Through the years, my "someday" book has gotten thicker.

For a few months, a child with autism attended our church and the mother so wanted him to take an interest in Sunday school. This beautiful child struggled with things out of his normal routine so the mother asked to stay in the classroom also. I assured her that her presence would be welcome.

We sat in a circle on the floor for story time and I began telling the children the Bible story for the day. As I spoke, this child began to mimic me and tell the story in his own way. At first I was startled, but then quickly realized as much as the mother tried to quiet him, he was going to tell the story too. He had trouble speaking clearly but that did not deter him. The other children gathered in the circle adjusted immediately to looking at me and then turning to look at this little boy for his interpretation. When the boy noticed the other children paying attention to him, he became even more animated and continued to rattle after me until I had completed the story. After class the mother thanked me and said they would be back and maybe he would be better. I assured her he was fine and I would see them next week.

As I turned to clean up our room, one other little boy had stayed behind. Bradley tugged on my skirt and said, "Miss Jill, I touldn't unnerstand a word that wittle boy said, but he really knowed that Bible tory!"

Bradley had no idea that he too was hard to understand or that his new little friend would have such a struggle in life. Isn't that just like a little child? He didn't understand the boy's words, but was accepting of their differences. Wouldn't this be a better place to live if we all accepted people, even if we didn't understand them?

One lovely lady in our church has five grandchildren and I have been the teacher of all five: Nicole, Zach, Quinn, Lexus and McKenzie. There are some characters in this bunch! Every Sunday when I headed into the sanctuary, the parents would wait in anticipation to see what their child had done or said in class that week.

For example, one day Nicole said, "Miss Jill guess what? Nana got a new car!"

"Oh, how exciting!" I exclaimed. "What color is it?"

"Chartreuse!"

Now most three-year-olds have no clue how to say that word, not to mention know that it was a color. But I played it cool and replied, "Oh how pretty! I love chartreuse, don't you?"

Then I quickly walked to the window to look out and see what color Nana's new car really was. Yep, you guessed it. Chartreuse!

One of the routines in our Sunday class was to use the restroom at the first bell so that none of the children would need to be excused during worship to visit the bathroom. Lexus, in fact, was so used to me taking her to the bathroom at church that even when there was any other function at church, and even if her mom or dad were at church, she would come seek me out to take her to the restroom. On one such occasion, I was speaking at a ladies banquet and Lexus felt the urge to go. She marched right up to the podium and stood right beside me. When I noticed her, I leaned down and said, "May I help you?"

"I need to go potty," she replied.

Well, what is a teacher to do but leave the ladies and take her to the restroom? I asked the ladies to talk amongst themselves and I would return shortly. Lexus' mother tried to intervene, but Lexus insisted that Miss Jill take her to the bathroom. We all had a good laugh and I went on with my talk.

Quinn was a handful. His daddy was military and when daddy was at drill over the weekend, Quinn's momma would drag him kicking and screaming to Sunday school. "I want my daddy" was heard loudly throughout the church building. As I would take Quinn from his mother so she could go to her class, I would usually hold him on my lap. Many times I would tell the Bible story with a sobbing Quinn getting snot all over my shirt. He would hiccup and his little lip would quiver.

"I want my daddy" he would say and look up at me with the saddest puppy dog eyes you would ever see. My response to him was always the same. "No more than I do, Quinn!" That I wanted his daddy seemed to pacify him and he would eventually join the rest of the children.

One of the children, who will remain nameless for privacy and embarrassment's sake asked me to do something I had never done before. We were having a Valentine party and this was his first official class activity. His dad brought him to the party and said, "Now, we are potty training ******** and he is doing pretty well, but when he says he has to go, he has to go right then!"

"Okay, no problem," I said with bravado. "So does he sit or stand?"

"He stands."

A couple of hours later and the class had all gathered around the table. We were finger painting big red and pink hearts when this little boy exclaims, "I gotta go!" So off we rush to the bathroom with his paint smock on and his two little hands covered in red paint, but raised to the sky so as to not touch anything.

"Let's wash your hands really quickly!" I said.

To which he replied, "Hurry!"

So we are quick about it and I unsnap his pants, lift the lid and have him assume the position. He stands there and stands there … with nothing happening. Then he begins to make small talk.

"I like to paint." I'm sure I smiled.

"My mommy will love her red heart I make. My bruder's is nice too." I probably nodded in agreement.

Finally, he looks up at me and asks, "Well are you gonna hold it?"

I stuttered and said, "Well I guess I can!"

So I did, and he immediately took care of his business. This poor little fellow had been waiting for me to "aim" him in the right direction, not wanting to make a mess.

"I think his potty training is going well," I told his dad when he returned. "You left a very important part of the instructions out and I will never let you forget it!"

McKenzie's father was military and as I said previously had not only weekend drills but also deployments. After 9/11 there had been a lot of news regarding the people of Iraq. During one of our Sunday morning prayer times, McKenzie asked God to help the "Iwacky" people.

Some of those Iraqi people were the reason her dad was gone, but she wanted God to help them.

Bradley was a sharp little boy. He would catch on to things quickly. His mother and I had been good friends since we started kindergarten together. We were out at the local pizza place one evening when Bradley's mom told a joke. While we all laughed, Bradley, (at age four) rolled his eyes and said loudly, "My mom is trying to be a Canadian!"

This "comedian" laughed even harder.

Carl was a little boy with a hard family life, and he was brought to church with his half- brother and sister by a neighbor lady. Carl blossomed under the attention he received in Sunday school and church. He listened intently as I told the Bible story each week.

During the Christmas season we talked about Jesus having the birthday, but we get the gift. I asked the children what they were going to give to Jesus this year for his birthday.

"Maybe you can give him your praise by singing in big church," I suggested. "Or maybe you can give him your service by helping someone here at church."

Our craft that day was to color a small picture of Mary, Joseph and baby Jesus that we would place inside a clear ornament. Carl colored his picture and I carefully inserted it into the ornament.

I said, "You can hang this on your tree this year Carl, to remember that Christmas is really Jesus's birthday."

Now before I finish the story you need to know that Carl never took his projects from church home. When I asked why, he simply stated that his mom would just "frow it away." So usually Carl would find someone in big church to give his project to. He didn't have to know the person well and would offer it to young or old alike. This endeared him to everyone at church. I sent Carl off to big church with his little ornament, thinking surely he would take this project home.

This Christmas season, like many others, we had a manger in the sanctuary with a small doll placed inside to represent the baby Jesus. Tucked inside that manger was Carl's ornament. He had listened to the story and had given Jesus a gift: his ornament.

Now I must confess that I took that ornament home, and my plan was to give it back to Carl when he was older. Remember, he had a rough family life? Well Carl's family went through another crisis, and this time, Carl and his dad and mom moved in one direction, his brother went to one family member, and his sister went to yet another. Carl moved to a new town and I no longer know where he lives or if he is safe. I often think of him and pray for his safety and pray that he knows he is loved by God and by many in our small church.

Each Christmas Carl's little ornament hangs on my tree. It reminds me of the privilege I have to teach such young lives and instill in them the love of God.

God had a plan for my life that didn't include biological children of my own. His plan included the beautiful children of my little town who I love like my own. He gave me the opportunity to mold and shape them as youngsters and to guide and advise them as youth and adults. He gave me lots of laughter and stories to tell. God gave me above and beyond what I could ask or imagine. I am still teaching preschool and love their honesty and zest to learn and help.

Oh, that we adults would have the mindset of a little child and soak up the stories of Jesus for the treasures they are. Every new bit of information learned brings them joy, and they love to tell someone about it. I love it when that someone is me. After all, isn't that how we enter the Kingdom of Heaven—like a little child?

–Jill McNicol

Out of the Woods

No drugs. No fighting. Food daily. How I got to this place is a very long story. I'll give you the abbreviated, PG-13 version.

I'd been drinking with people—adults, and got charged with illegal consumption. The officers let me go, but when you are a drunk teenager, being influenced by drunk adults, you do stupid things. Within a few hours, I got caught again, and had to spend a night in jail.

Twenty-six days later, I found myself going through alcohol withdrawal in a coed, adolescent foster home. The shaking, cold, puking, and diarrhea weren't enough to convince me that I was a sixteen-year-old addict.

"I've got the flu. Leave me alone," I told the counselors.

I ran away with a few of the girls, but they found us and brought us back. Now, I'm slapped with the identities of both an alcoholic and a runaway. Other labels suited me, too. Rebellious, wild, and strong-willed. I'd been tumbling in a cycle of creating new problems in an attempt to escape the old ones. I had plenty to escape from, and narrow escapes make life exciting. Right?

They made us runaways wear crazy outfits and confiscated our shoes. The humiliation served only to make me angry. When we could no longer tolerate the strict rules and the "counseling," three of us ran again. We thought we were smart, leaving right after breakfast with no coats or shoes on a chilly November 30 in Illinois.

We'd planned to run through the woods until we got to town. When the first shot was fired, one of the girls laughed and said, "Deer hunting season!"

There's nothing like a gunshot, in a heavily wooded area, to cause you to turn in confusion and lose the sense of direction you never really had in the first place. We weren't walking now. We were runaways, and running hard. Our feet were wet, cold and already bleeding, but we couldn't take time to notice. We stopped only to catch our breath, then took off in a direction that seemed opposite the gunfire. The shots were infrequent and random. I wished for a drink to calm the terror.

"This could be worse," one of the girls said. "It could be the police."

Low hanging branches scraped our faces and arms. Broken twigs and tree roots tore into the flesh of our feet. Stepping on something as small as a smooth stone caused me to stop suddenly for a painful reflex that jerked a knee to my chest. I didn't cry. I believed we were nearing the edge of the woods, and I wasn't the kind of girl who admitted defeat, so I took the next step. A thousand next steps later, and we still hadn't found a clearing.

Around noon, the hunters had either shot their limit or given up and left the area. With no clue where we were going, and nothing to eat or drink, we headed into the afternoon hours, denying that our plan had been flawed.

The three of us began to slow our pace and discuss what we should do, not for the next hour or for the rest of the day, but for our immediate safety and survival. We couldn't come to an agreement on the best action, except that we needed to stay together. I quietly repeated, "Never again." I wouldn't have been able to state exactly when it was that my life went wrong, and the video playing in my mind did not help me determine what it was that I would never do again.

With dusk in process, my heart rate quickened. We had passed the same tree three times or more. The throbbing spread from my feet to my calves and thighs. Then, we saw lights and a trailer park.

One of the trailers was obviously abandoned, but locked. We broke in. It had no furniture, water or heat, and most of the windows were missing. Trash and other paraphernalia cluttered the place. The three of us were not the first to use this hangout. We ripped curtains from their rods to use as blankets.

The next morning, we drank water from rain puddles, and I ventured far enough away from the others to think and develop a new plan. An elderly lady agreed to let me use her phone.

"Our car broke down. I need to call my mom."

I wonder now if she wasn't afraid of the filthy and stinky, shoeless girl who walked with a limp. The smoothest and softest of surfaces against the soles of my feet caused pain. Repeating "thank-you," each time with a wide smile, probably led the old lady to feel sorry for me and take a risk. She handed me her phone.

Mom said she would come get me, but she also called the police. Fifteen hours of waiting at the police station should have been enough time to reflect on how I would never be in such a mess again. It wasn't.

Mom finally showed. I met her as an in-control and independent teen who only needed a ride home. She heard about the rude cops and the overly hostile foster parents and counselors at the adolescent home.

I had escaped, narrowly and painfully, but I escaped.

My troubles were put into perspective when Mom gave me the news that some of my friends were in a car wreck while I was away. The wreck had been a result of drinking and driving. One of them had died.

He was my stepdad's ex-stepson, and my friend. I felt grief over the loss of a friend as well as some loss of my own youthful invincibility. When Mom and I got home, my step-dad met me at the door. He picked me up into his arms and held me. I'd never experienced anything like that from him. He made me feel wanted.

My cycle of sin and narrow escape slowed after that experience in the woods, but I was still spinning. Some of the sins came out of my own nature and choosing. However, on many occasions when I would have chosen to end the chaos, someone else's sin, usually an adult, reached out and gave me another whirl.

And the cycle didn't start with the person who had provided the alcohol at the beginning of this episode. Back then, if there was a hotline for people who were being trafficked into the sex trade, I didn't know it. Running into the woods ended up saving my life.

My family situation had always been far from the ideal. Not in any particular order, but my parents fought a lot and drank a lot. Getting out of the house was something I looked forward to. All I wanted was to be loved and safe. Mom and Dad were caught in a cycle of their own.

A lady named Maurine started picking us kids up and taking us to 4H meetings. I loved 4H, and I loved Maurine. She invited us in whenever we knocked on her door. I think she felt sorry for us. Soon, she was taking us to church.

Other people at the church made me feel cared for and protected, but the time always came for us to go home. One Sunday, as we sang the song, "Just

As I Am," I went in front of all those people to tell the pastor that I believed in Jesus. We prayed, and I really did believe.

Between the ages of nine and thirteen, we moved several times. (My parents were runaways of a different sort.) Not much changed, except that in every town we moved to, I had to find a church, and get there. I didn't care about school, but I wanted to be in church.

Dad tried to kill himself many times, usually because Mom tired of the beatings and had left. One might think a child could build an immunity to the repeated drama, but that wasn't my experience. I "got" scared every time. I prayed and hoped God would hear me. Along with the alcohol, Mom and Dad used speed. They had done if for years, but had managed to hide it from us kids until I was about eleven years old. Then, I started using too. Getting high was easy, and I needed escape as much as any adult.

I remember hiding in a closet with my mom, brother, sister and a cousin. People were just outside our house, threatening to kill our family over a drug deal gone wrong. Dad and my uncle "got" a beating that nearly killed them.

Dad "got" caught driving under the influence and his driver's license "got" revoked. He "got" drunk, again, and insisted on driving. Mom ran out to the car in her bare feet, trying to stop him.

She reached in through the car window and tried to take the keys. He rolled the window up and trapped her arm. There was my mother, being dragged about in a parking lot, gravel and dust flying from under the back tires. She "got" hurt bad, and I was helpless to stop it.

I remember the happy drinking and drug parties where all the adults (and some of the kids) "got" wasted or high, but many of those parties ended with yelling and fighting. That word "got" is such a passive verb, and where I came from, nobody ever "got" anything good.

God didn't answer my prayers the way I asked. Mom finally left us for a long time, and when I saw her again, I had a step-dad. I didn't blame her for choosing to leave. I prayed for her every day.

Dad's "award" in the divorce was his children. He overdosed again, so we stayed with his parents. I got to be more than they could handle, so Mom took me back. Different houses, different schools (when I went), and different churches. No day was predictable. My step-dad's brother took me to live with his family, where I went to church and wanted to belong. I felt like such a sinner, and acted like one, too. I was old enough to know when I was guilty of a sin and confess it to God, but discouraged and frustrated with my attempts to be a "good person." The younger kids in the house did not need me around.

A cousin, who was already a foster parent, took me in until the state of Illinois investigated because I had missed so much school. They threatened to remove the other foster kids from the home.

Then my dad had a car crash, which was awful because he broke his arm in three places, broke his neck and was in a coma for three months. The awfulness was multiplied because we heard, in real time on a police scanner, all the events leading up to the wreck. A gun, a couple of hostages, a house being shot up and a high-speed police chase involving multiple counties was played for us to hear. Dad recovered and was able to return to work, but the law caught up with him, and he went to prison.

Friends introduced me to marijuana in the fifth grade. I wanted to fit in somewhere. I still skipped school, but looked forward to church.

Hearing stories about faith, exciting rescues, and miraculous changes of heart kept me going back to church. I went as often as I could, but Mom and my step-dad wouldn't go, except to be married there. I asked permission to be baptized, but Mom said, "No."

My step-dad wasn't a nice man, and he was even meaner when he was coming down from a drug high. I didn't exactly help his disposition. I knew him to be the one who took my mother from my father and broke our family. He was, after all, supposed to have been my dad's best friend. I returned meanness as often as I could find opportunity.

Dad had told me hundreds of times not to trust him, and I didn't. The man needed drugs more than anything and seemed to enjoy beating on people. He put Mom's life in some serious danger on a regular basis. Sometimes, as Mom's guardians, us kids watched. Other times we were unwilling participants. Us kids heard and saw a lot of bad adult behavior. I was afraid of him, and wasn't ashamed of my reputation as his enemy.

He drove a semi. We'd never quite heal from his last episode, when he'd walk through the door again. Not that all was peaceful and lovey-dovey when he was on the road.

Mom tried. I saw how she wanted a better life, but couldn't manage to get there. It seemed that absolutely no one was on her side. I went to church and knew there was a better way to live, a way we ought to live, and that caused me to be confused and frustrated. Mom and I weren't much help to each other, except as occasional crying buddies.

Eventually, she didn't know what to do with me. Neither of us really knew how to act or get out of our situation. My plan was always to survive until I turned eighteen, with or without her help. I couldn't live in her house with my step-dad there.

I stayed with any family member who would take me in, which I'm sure was a headache to the state's caseworkers. I did what I could to make them earn their paychecks. They placed me with my grandparents again until Grandpa had his leg amputated due to diabetes. His health had declined in general, and it was too much for Grandma to handle both Grandpa and me.

My brother and sister had aged out of the system, but that meant another foster home for me. I loved it there. No drugs, no fights and food daily. Of course, it couldn't last. Three other foster girls were the grandkids of our foster parents. We got along great, and it was going well until I wasn't allowed to go where I wanted to go, or do what I wanted to do. The other kids came from messed up parents and bad situations too, but it looked to me as though they were being treated better than me. I was jealous. They had grandparents, and other things I'd never have.

A weekend visit with another family turned out good. We went skating and I got to play games, be a kid, and hang out with other real kids. Still, I felt awkward and unwanted.

Every possible relative had taken me in at least once during my fourteen years. My aunt took me back, again. She was super nice and had nice things, although she wasn't one to buy groceries and cook. There were other teens in the house, and it was a cool place to be. That's where I found this boy … or maybe he found me. Neither of us were closely supervised, and although it was uncomfortable, I let him talk me into doing things I knew to be wrong.

I got used to being independent at the age of fifteen, and that's when another conflict started. All of a sudden, my aunt started taking control of her own household and demanded to know of my coming and goings. There was a battle anytime she said "No."

The next foster parents were strict from day one. They chose which clothes we would wear and what time we did everything. We did more than what I'd been used to as household chores. Far more. All of us kids referred to ourselves as slaves, as their punishments were so harsh.

I called Mom and told her what was going on. She reported to D.C.F.S. (The Department of Children and Family Services). I would have been removed from the home, along with the other kids, but I ran before the investigation took place. I wasn't fine, but I knew how to hide—from D.C.F.S that is.

My story, as you've probably figured out, takes me to a place where adult men were "giving" me a roof over my head and a place to sleep. I paid a price for any other needs, comforts or privileges. Substances seemed to help. Again, creating a new problem in an attempt to escape the old one. I always had a plan for escaping, but today was never the right time.

That night in jail might just have been a good thing. God put those hunters in those woods on that chilly November 30 for me. Sometimes a memory is all you need to keep straight.

It's scary, telling my story. PG-13 version or not. Friends that didn't know me in my younger days sometimes tell me I should write a book. My favorite chapter (a long one) would be about how God moved me from danger and created a family where now I'm the mom, loving kids of my own.

I've never been able to tell my entire story in one, two or three sittings, but wherever my story begins or wraps-up, I always want people to know (especially young girls) that I came "out of the woods." I love telling just how God made that happen.

God rescued Mom too, but not until she'd spent some time in prison for a drug conviction. A man was also guilty, but as it often happens, he did not get incarcerated. In recent years, Mom and I have done some growing up together. We have a mother-daughter story that needs to be written someday.

Not long ago, I took my teen daughter to visit a home where girls with problems are cared for and loved. We went with some ladies from our church to do a craft and fix a meal with them. Part of the plan was to encourage the girls with a Bible story and to share something of our own lives. Terrifying!

My fumbling and blubbering through much of my talk didn't seem to matter to the girls. At the end, I'd done my best to point them to Jesus. I saw tears, and there were hugs. All of those girls were on the edge of their "woods" and some of them had just spotted the clearing.

–Dawn Wright

He Said Go. I Went

As a teenager, I attended a weekend youth retreat with my church. The speaker was a dynamic missionary who had been called to minister in Africa. His wife talked about helping the women give birth in the middle of a straw hut and he showed a video about digging trenches for miles to bring water to the village. I was fascinated by their stories, and I couldn't take my eyes off the images of the dark eyed children in their photos. But in my heart I kept saying, "Lord, please don't send me to Africa!" Many years later, I was in my first year of marriage and God was clearly calling my husband, David, to a rural church in southern Illinois.

I grew up in Kansas City surrounded by family and friends. I taught middle school in the same district I grew up in. I bought a house within walking distance of my grandparents. My family had dinner together every Wednesday night. My extended family got together for every little holiday and birthday. When we first started dating, David was amused at how rooted my family and I were. He grew up as a pastor's kid and attended eight different schools between kindergarten and high school, then worked in five different states between high school and meeting me, so moving was second nature to him. Moving away from Kansas City had never even occurred to me until I met David.

When we first started dating, David had recently stepped away from being a full-time pastor to pursue his doctorate degree in Kansas City. Early in our relationship, he casually mentioned over dinner that part of being in a relationship with him could include moving. I nonchalantly said I would do whatever God called us to and continued eating my chicken Alfredo. In our first year of marriage, David worked as a teacher at a Christian high school, but he still felt the call to be a full-time pastor. He prayerfully watched job postings, filled in as needed for pastors on Sundays, and trusted that God would lead him to a church when the time was right. About a year into our marriage, that time had come.

The first time I stepped into the small church was for David's initial interview. Part of being a pastor's wife means that you get to tag along while the search committee asks your husband about his theological beliefs, leadership traits, and thoughts on various ministries. The search committee was incredibly kind and welcoming. They treated us to lunch at a small diner that featured home cooking and the most delicious chocolate chess pie you've ever had. (I quickly learned that every good meal in southern Illinois would end with pie.) A few weeks later, the church voted unanimously to call David as their pastor. We drove home to Kansas City and the realization of this decision settled in. I'm not going to lie, there were many tears, some silence, and a lot of thinking. *What have I gotten myself into?*

The church graciously allowed us to finish the school year in Kansas City since we were both teachers, so we had about eight weeks to prepare for the move. The next eight weeks were spent going through every item we owned, having a huge garage sale, and selling the house I had renovated with my dad eight years earlier. I loved that house, and I didn't want to move. I had to resign from the job I held for nine years and say goodbye to the many coworkers who were my good friends and confidants. I had no desire to live six hours from my parents, siblings, nephews, niece, and extended family, but I knew God was calling us to this church.

Growing up in Sunday school, I learned the story of Jonah and the whale. I remember thinking how silly Jonah was to disobey God's command to go to Nineveh. Now I was less judgmental of Jonah. I related to him on a level I wasn't prepared for. David will tell you that there were a couple of times during that eight weeks between accepting the call from the church and moving that he thought he was going to have to call the church and tell them that we wouldn't be coming. But like I said, I *knew* God was calling, so even though I didn't want to and it hurt my heart to leave everything I knew, we went.

That first weekend at the church was a whirlwind. Everyone was giving hugs, shaking hands, telling me back stories that I would never remember, and I still wasn't sure if this was real. We had dinner invitations, lunches brought to us, and more help moving than I knew what to do with. The congregation was incredibly gracious to us, and I'm forever grateful for their kindness.

I slowly started adapting to my new life. I got a job teaching at a small high school in the next county over where my students would tease me about saying "you all" instead of "y'all." I learned to leave for work ten minutes early during planting season in the spring and harvest in the fall because I was bound to get caught behind a combine or two. I got used to living thirty minutes from Walmart and not having a single fast food restaurant in our entire county. When we went to the nearest metropolitan area a little over an hour away, I reveled in getting a Starbucks drink, something I used to do every other day on the way to work.

When people asked me how I was doing, I would joke, "I always told God not to send me to Africa, but I never said anything about not sending me to the middle of nowhere!" They say God won't lead you to anything you can't handle, but in reality I couldn't handle being a pastor's wife in a small town where I didn't know anyone. I still can't handle the critical comments from church members toward my husband. I can't handle the raised expectations that come with being a pastor's wife. Thankfully though, God can and He does.

–Jenny Auxier

Stolen Joy

"Grandma Rita! Grandma Rita! Brother did a real bad sin! Shoved the game right off the table, I was just about to win!"

Times like these it takes a Grandma to discern the wrong and right, step between two angry children, heal the hurt and stop a fight. All day long the girl asks Grandma, "Just what sin did he commit?"

They would look to find the answer. "Both of you come here and sit."

As she opened up her Bible, precious child on either side, a quick prayer went up to heaven asking Jesus to abide.

"Let's read from the *Ten Commandments*. Moses got these words from God."

Grandma knew His Word had power, yet was gentler than the rod. As she read, the siblings listened with a friendly rivalry. Who would be the first to answer? Which commandment would it be?

The next verse, "Obey your parents."

Would this be the one they'd choose? Calculating stare between them; hinted that someone would lose. Grandma Rita had a moment when she wondered what she'd done. *Lord, I fear that when I've finished, one has lost, the other won.* Once again, God offered mercy. Saved her from a dreadful pain.

Verse fifteen, from chapter twenty, Brother said, "Read that again."

"Do not steal."

He contemplated. Smart, but still a little boy. Then a most profound confession.

"Grandma Rita, I stole her joy."

In the prayers upon her pillow, Grandma has a lot to say, but that night she mostly listened for more lessons from the day. Better than her morning coffee, was the peace that she could feel, with the game back on the table, children saying, "We won't steal."

"Grandma tell us, did you ever do a sin as bad as steal? Or was something stolen from you? From your heart or something real?"

Grandma thought for just a minute, placed a finger on her brow. Yes, she'd had a few things taken. Memories flooded back, just now.

"Once a purse with grocery money, and there was a radio."

"Grandma Rita! Grandma Rita! What important things you stole!"

"No! Those things were taken from me. Not the other way around, but there's thievery within me. I'm embarrassed when it's found. I've been guilty. Stole some glory. Grandpa might tell you a tale, but for sure I've never taken anything deserving jail."

Grandma Rita told more stories of how stealing causes grief. She made sure they got the message that our God still loves the thief.

"Mommy's pulling up the driveway. Do we really have to go?"

Socks and shoes. "Where is your homework?"

"In my backpack, don't you know?"

Rita felt a little saddened. Time with grandkids was all done, then she heard them say to Mommy, "That new game was loads of fun."

–Rita Klundt

A Thousand Second Chances

"Another couple of hours, and we wouldn't be having this conversation. It would be too late." My husband, Larry, my mom, my brother, and my sister-in-law heard what the doctor said, but no one told me. I was in the recovery room waking up from anesthesia, still in pain.

It was well after midnight by now, and this was a different kind of pain than what had prompted me to call my small-town doctor the day before. With this pain, a kind nurse was handy to deliver fast-acting relief. She hinted that I had been through a "serious" surgery, but nothing was said about what might have happened if I had waited a few hours before calling the doctor or if I had ignored his medical advice.

The medication allowed me rest from the pain and scattered periods of sleep during the next few hours. For that, I was grateful.

Then it was daylight. The bandage on my abdomen served to remind me of yesterday's pain, several unfinished tasks, and some personal responsibilities that now would belong to someone else. I began to create mental lists. The community fundraiser would begin in a few hours, without me. Friends, and a few strangers, would understand and carry on, but that brought me little comfort. Pain had rearranged a few schedules without my permission. For the next several days, a gaping surgical wound would dictate my level of activity and interaction with the outside world, but I was mentally reviewing the events of the past twenty-four hours.

It hadn't been an everyday pain. When I say "it felt like a thousand needles stabbing me in the side," I mean big needles. Jagged needles. The pain worsened, and none of my home remedies brought relief. Our country doctor answered the phone within a few rings. He must not have had a patient in the office. It was just him—no office staff or nurse. I told him about the pain, and how nothing I'd tried would make it go away. "I need something for pain."

He denied my request. "You need to either come to the office or get yourself to the emergency room."

I explained my situation and was laying out a plan that included him calling in a prescription for now, and then holding a spot for me on his schedule for an office visit later in the afternoon, after I had dealt with all the things on my to-do list.

The doctor was not persuaded. "You need to either come to the office now or get yourself to the emergency room."

I knew enough not to drive myself, so I called a good friend for a ride. A doctor visit would be closer and faster than the ER, but I stuck to my plan for picking up a prescription, popping a pill in the car, and continuing with my day, my way.

The doctor greeted me with, "So you're having some belly pain. What's going on?"

I repeated the "thousands of needles" description, including my commitment to the fundraiser. "If I could have something for the pain, I think I can make it?"

"You look a little dehydrated. Up on the table."

"Up on the table? Does he have any idea how much this hurts?"

He poked around my belly button. "Does this hurt?"

"No."

"How about this?" he asked.

"Oh yeah. That hurts!" It was less of an answer to his exact question and more a warning not to poke me there again. My words supported my body language as I sat up and guarded my abdomen.

"You're going to the emergency room. Something's going on in there. We can't take care of it here in the office." He called the hospital ER. I called Larry to let him know where my day was going and that his day wasn't looking too good either.

The emergency room nurse started with questions, checking my vital signs and attaching wires. I made sure she knew I needed something for my pain. The couple of needles she stuck in my elbow were nothing in comparison to the ones still attacking me from the inside. The medical student who came in next was nice enough, but he didn't have the authority to order pain medication, which is what really mattered to me.

Finally, someone with the initials M.D. behind his name came in to examine me. He was confirming what had been reported to him by my family doctor and the ER nurse as he pressed around on my abdomen. I was answering his questions and demonstrating patience, until he pressed hard on the same "spot." My reaction ended the exam, and he turned to the nurse and ordered pain medication.

I was wheeled to radiology for an x-ray and a sonogram. The ER doctor had already explained the course of action for gall stones, and the laparoscopic procedure, which would be "minimally invasive." We waited for a report.

It seemed that every ten minutes or so someone was asking, "On a scale from one to ten, how bad is it?"

"Fifteen."

The nurse kept the medication coming. In spite of the fact that I felt loopy and incapable of managing a simple conversation. My belly now hurt through to my side. By now, I had scrapped the day's schedule. When the doctor decided to check my abdomen for a second time, perhaps as a test of the medication's true effect, I didn't have the wherewithal to warn him. But, when he poked "the spot" I reacted.

"Your gallbladder looks good. No problem there."

He seemed satisfied with the radiologist's report, except now he had no explanation for my pain. There was talk about sending me home after extra fluids to flush the narcotics from my system. However, it was decided that I would be admitted for observation (and starvation) overnight. "We'll see how you feel in the morning," he said.

My family doctor got the same report and wasn't satisfied. He ordered another test. This one included drinking a white liquid, and a scan. Just how a scan is different from an x-ray, I'm not sure. It was all explained to me, but I was under the influence. We waited for the liquid to get to where it was going. Then, I waited for my turn with the huge camera. Larry and I waited some more, for a report. The pain kept getting worse. *How many needles would I need to say were stabbing me before somebody did something?*

Larry stayed with me until he couldn't keep his eyes open. We had passed most of our morning in the emergency room, all of our afternoon with medical testing, and our evening had turned to night. He told the nurse I needed another dose of pain medication before he left for home and a short night's rest in our own bed.

Our pastor came to visit me shortly after Larry left. It was almost midnight.

"You shouldn't have come! It's so late. I'll be going home in the morning."

When the phone interrupted my telling of the day's events, I considered not answering. We both asked, "Who would be calling at this time of night?"

My family doctor had reviewed all the tests and had some news for me. "It's your appendix. I've talked to a surgeon. He's on his way."

I started to question, but he interrupted. "This is going to happen tonight."

I called Larry to return to the hospital, and just like my doctor said, the nurses began to crowd into my room and prepare me for surgery. He somehow managed to make it to the hospital, along with my mom, my brother and his wife, before they wheeled me away. I imagined there hadn't been much traffic and no time was wasted searching for a parking space in the wee hours of the morning.

Hospital workers were so nice, and wide awake, considering the hour. I remember the transporters and the thinly padded cart that would take me to surgery. I heard an apology for every bump in the hallway. I was paying attention to the pattern on the curtains, the number of ceiling tiles per patient area, the texture of the heated blanket they used to cover me and other silly and non-essential details. Except for the staff in the surgical area assigned to care for me, the place was empty.

The surgeon introduced himself as we rounded the corner of the operating room. He wasn't quite so cheerful, but at least he was awake and spoke with confidence. He quickly summarized his plan for a laparoscopic procedure, but mentioned the possibility of opening my abdomen. I listened while I imagined a parking space, close to a private hospital entrance, with the surgeon's name on it. *How else could he have arrived so quickly? And what did he say his name is?*

And then, I was waking up in the recovery room. The nurse who used the term "serious" when speaking of my surgical procedure was hovering and adjusting my bed linens. I know she said some things, but nothing was said about what would have happened if my surgery had been delayed.

I saw my doctor, the surgeon, multiple nurses, and family members every day during the week I was hospitalized. But none of them told me I would likely have died if my surgery had been delayed another couple of hours.

I had dressing changes twice daily, but none of the nurses mentioned how close I came to death. Each doctor opened the dressing to have a peek at my wound every day, but my close call with death was old news to them. They said nothing to me.

Due to a terrible infection, my appendectomy incision was not stitched or stapled closed. It was covered with a light bandage, but left wide open to promote healing from the inside out. I had drains and tubes in odd places, all of which came with a rationale and some sort of teaching or warning.

"My appendix burst and there was a tear in my intestine," I explained for some of the nurses as they saw my wound for the first time and seemed repulsed. I informed a few nursing students as well.

There was no lack of attention to my needs. I was well cared for, but nothing was said, or even suggested about what might have happened if I had pushed through the pain and continued with my plans for the fundraiser, or if my family doctor had sent me home instead of to the emergency room. What if he hadn't been so proactive after turning my care over to the emergency room physician?

My nurses taught Larry (who never could bring himself to change a baby's messy diaper) to irrigate, repack, and dress a wound that made some of them gag. We had to be prepared for at least seven more weeks of healing at home. Larry's affectionate and tender devotion to caring for me was so different from what I had seen before. I knew he loved me, but this man had previously been unable to handle the unpleasantness of any sickness involving bodily fluids. He became my primary caregiver and home care nurse. In hindsight, his change of attitude and fortitude of character could have been because he knew how close he'd come to being widowed with children.

The surgeon had shared a photograph, taken during surgery, as an illustration of damage done by a ruptured appendix. The photo had an impact on Larry. He described the image with colorful detail to me—several times during the weeks he cared for my wound, but mentioned nothing of what the doctor had told him while I was in the recovery room.

My wound was finally closed, and healing well. The pain was gone, and I was approaching my baseline state of health. Weeks later, at a regular check-up, my doctor happened to mention that he had presented my case during a mortality and morbidity conference. He seemed to want me to know how sick I'd been, but nothing was said about death or dying. It was nice to be thought of as interesting and unique, but to me, the drama was over.

Fifteen years later, when the topic of my appendectomy became part of a casual conversation, Larry quoted the doctor's words. "Another couple of hours, and we wouldn't be having this conversation. It would be too late."

"I almost died, and no one told me?"

"You knew."

"No I didn't. I would remember if the doctor told me something like that!"

We figured that everyone thought someone else had told me. The reality is that it never mattered what I knew. It only mattered that my doctor knew. He was the one in charge. But, I found myself repeating (sometimes audibly), "I almost died!"

I don't know that my years of being uninformed changed one thing, but learning how near I'd been to death caused me to think of other second chances. None of us can report the number of times we've been to the brink of death, and been rescued by God. We oversleep, leave late for work and see the terrible accident that could have involved us. We get the red light instead of a yellow. We pick up a nasty germ, but wash it from our hands before it finds a way to our eyes, nose or mouth. What about those busy and lethal microscopic organisms that make others dreadfully sick, but have no ill effect on us? Second chances must happen all the time.

Our preschool-aged son woke us early one morning with his crying. We both tended to him because this cry was different. I had some difficulty getting out of bed and struggled with my balance. Larry had a headache. Our oldest son slept undisturbed. Unbeknownst to us, a bird had built a nest in the chimney, and carbon monoxide had been filling our home while we slept.

I was already lightheaded and foggy minded. Larry managed to direct me and the boys downstairs, and in spite of his headache, he went about preparing to go to work.

Maybe it was the bit of fresh air that rushed the room when Larry opened the door and left the house. The concentration of carbon monoxide might have been heavier in the upstairs bedrooms. Either way, I began to feel better and expected my usual routine would resume after a bit more rest.

Two hours later, both of the boys were sleeping. Something had caused me to wake after dozing in my chair. It was a struggle to crawl along the floor and get to the phone, but I wouldn't have been able to stand or coordinate my steps.

The emergency room doctor was exceedingly clear that carbon monoxide poisoning would have taken the lives of both our sons and myself. Except for that "something" that woke us, we would have died.

Our van had trouble starting a few weeks ago. I was inconvenienced and upset for anticipating the cost of a new battery or starter. When a gas leak turned out to be the problem, I forgot about any inconvenience or expense. I was humbled instead, that God would look at my life with such detail and care.

The mechanic left little to our imaginations. He warned, "I can't let you drive this van one mile until you get this line replaced. With a gas leak like this and a hot engine …"

My baby granddaughter is a frequent passenger. The what-ifs consumed the rest of my day and most of my week. *How long had that line been leaking? How many miles had I driven without knowing the danger? I smelled gasoline when I started the van a week ago! How could I have ignored that? How long does it take me to get her out of that crazy car seat? What if …?*

I'm not ready to tally all my second chances. It would be impossible, and I don't think God rescues us to keep us indebted by His mercies, seen or unseen. I'm not sure if I should call them second chances or miracles.

We are supposed to thank God for His goodness and protection without fearing what might not happen. We ought to praise Him for His love and all-knowing ways without taking Him for granted.

Yes, I'm sure I've had a thousand second chances.

–Sandra Taylor

My Name is Marilyn

"I don't have a story."

"Sure you do," she said.

"Nope."

And the lady started asking questions, but not until we had watched the last fifteen minutes of *Wheel of Fortune*. The contestant didn't figure out the phrase in the bonus round, and neither did we. $37,000. "That's a lot of money to lose," she said.

"I love it when they win."

Chet muted the TV and leaned back in his recliner. He was more excited about telling my story than I was. I've had three strokes, and since then, his mouth always moves faster than mine. I have a good husband. The lady said she was writing a book and wanted to include a story about me. She started the interview by asking my birthday. What that had to do with my story, I don't know.

"Fifty-three."

"You were born in 1953?" she asked.

Chet grabbed the armrests and pulled himself to a sitting position. I knew I already got something wrong. "No. You're not fifty-three. You're seventy–three!"

The lady laughed and said, "You would have gotten by with that if Chester (that's what some people call my husband) wasn't sitting right here!"

I still didn't know what on earth she could write about me that would interest anyone, and then she asked me to tell her about my first stroke.

"I don't remember."

"She was in the hospital for twelve days." Chet remembered. "We woke up one morning and she couldn't talk. Her words were slow and slurred. Her left side, what little she could move, was weak. That was a rough twelve days. We don't ever want to do that again."

"Marilyn, do you remember anything about that first stroke?"

"Nope. Only what he tells me to remember."

"And the second stroke. Do you remember anything about how that happened?"

I had an answer, although I wasn't sure it would be right, but I couldn't think of a word to get a sentence started. Chet volunteered to tell her.

"That one was only two days after she got home from the hospital with the first stroke. I'd been out mowing the yard, and when I came inside, she was sitting in her recliner, leaning to her side, and the same thing was happening when she tried to talk."

"So, you had another ambulance ride?"

"Yep," I said. "All three times. I rode in an ambulance."

"But you don't remember?" she asked.

"Nope."

"You remember some of it," Chet said. "Like all that therapy."

I remember the therapy. That was hard.

Chet kept talking. "She had a lot of therapy. She doesn't go anywhere without that cane, but at first, she needed two people to help her get from the bed to a chair!"

I reached out and patted the handle of my quad cane like some people would pat an old dog. You know, like it's a nuisance sometimes, but I sure do depend on it and don't know what I'd do without it. "I get wobbly when I walk. And my hands shake. This one is worse." I held out my left hand and showed her my tremor. "I don't carry hot coffee."

The lady nodded and jotted a note on her tablet. "And then you had a third stroke?"

I don't mind questions, and nobody takes much interest in my story anymore. Lately, all anybody is talking about is that COVID virus … on the news and just about everywhere. Which I don't know about everywhere, but I have gone to the doctor's office, and lately, Chet and I have been to McDonald's and The Cracker Barrel. We don't go a lot of places. We like to go to church.

Chet told her about my third stroke. "That was a bad one. I found her on the bed, like she passed out and fell over, right there on the bed. She was totally out. Pretty scary. I couldn't get her to wake up at all."

The lady nodded and waited for Chet to continue. She glanced at me, but Chet was doing a good job telling her everything. Besides, I don't remember. He gets real serious-like when he says the part that I "almost died."

"By now, you probably knew what was happening," the lady said.

Chet didn't say anything right away. When it takes him a few seconds to start talking, he's thinking about what someone just said. When it takes me a while to start talking, I'm trying to remember a word. Chet didn't answer her question directly.

"She almost died. But then she started to come around, a little bit every day."

"And lots more therapy?"

"Oh yeah. I'm proud of how hard she worked. She had a great attitude."

Chet says that now, but I do remember some things. He was a big nag; pushing and dragging me to therapy when I wanted to sleep. I have a good husband, but I could've choked him a time or two. He went on to tell her about the different kinds of therapy I'd had. Physical therapy, where they taught me to walk again. Occupational therapy, where they helped me get my hands to work, and of course speech therapy. I had to learn how to swallow food and talk. Actually, that helped me remember my words.

"If you think my speech is slow now, you didn't know me back then," I said.

The lady set her pen down, looked up and just listened. She didn't ask about what caused my strokes, which is kind of surprising because she's a nurse. Chet told her though.

"All that stress!"

"Stress?"

"Her job. They treated her awful. Something new every day."

I didn't know what that had to do with anything. The lady kept nodding, her hand playing with her pen, but she didn't pick it up, and Chet kept talking.

"Her bosses hounded her to do the work that the younger people were too lazy to do. She didn't talk back like one of those kids would have. Less stress for the boss that way, but Marilyn, she shouldn't have been bullied like that."

I agreed.

"Marilyn. I know there are some things you can't or don't do since you had the strokes, but tell me, is there anything you really miss?"

I didn't even need to think before answering. "I don't miss work."

She chuckled and smiled.

"Then, is there something you wish were different?"

"I don't have any regrets."

"No regrets?"

"Nope."

Early on, I had a few regrets, but I don't remember them now. At my age (not 53), I'd be retired from work anyway. My life isn't that different from a lot of women. I make my bed every morning, I do laundry and I cook a little. In fact, I've got it a lot better than some people. I've got Chet, and he does all the hard stuff.

I was beginning to wonder what my story might read like once it is in a book. I thought, boring. Then she asked, "How did the two of you meet?"

Chet's not a bad storyteller, but he isn't that great either. He started talking and I felt my face getting warm. I trusted him not to get too personal, and he didn't, but boy oh boy, do I remember those days. I wouldn't go on a date with Chet, or any guy, by myself. But I agreed to go, if another girl would come along. I can't tell you what I had for breakfast, but I can tell you about that Mercury Comet! A white, 1965, two-door hardtop. He got four speeding tickets that year and lost his license for a few months. He blamed it on the car having four barrels. I never did see any barrels. They were under the hood. Chet loved that car. Everything a guy his age would want—a good job, a sporty new car, cash in his pocket, he had everything but a good woman. That's why he liked me.

I liked him too.

Not long before that date, my life had taken a turn for the good. Since the day my mother dropped me off on Grandma's front porch, I'd been in foster care, and Chet was telling this writer all about it. She didn't ask me any questions about those years, other than to agree, "That must have been hard. I had no idea!"

The lady interviewing me (us) is in our Sunday morning Bible class, and she wouldn't know that part of my story. Chet and I don't talk about ourselves much, and hardly anyone ever asks. Until this interview, I didn't know she has three children, a boy and two girls. Just this evening, we figured out that we're both proud parents of a lieutenant coronel. My daughter is in the United States Air Force, and her son recently retired from the United States Marine Corp.

I was glad she didn't ask a lot of questions about my childhood. All I told her was, "I had a rough life." What happened when I was two, or four, or fourteen years old isn't important anymore. Some things, I wish I didn't remember. If we had talked all night I couldn't have told her the worst of it. She listened to Chet as he told her a few things, but she wasn't taking notes.

She must've been done asking questions, because she eyed my crochet basket. "You crochet."

"Yep." I shrugged and, with a wave of my right hand, let her know how little I appreciated my own work.

"You should see some of the throws and blankets she's made. Pretty fancy. She crocheted an American flag as big as a bedspread!" Chet added, "Now, she only remembers a few of those stiches, but she still does a real good job. I'm proud of her."

I reached for a small afghan that I'd finished a few days earlier. "Here, I want you to have this."

"You don't need to do that."

"I want to. I want you to have it."

"Well then, thank you," she said. "This will be a nice throw to use in my office chair."

She thanked me for sharing my story and asked, "Is it alright if I come back sometime? I might want another story."

"Sure."

Chet added, "Come back anytime."

I think he enjoyed her visit as much as I did, especially when she got him to talk about that '65 Mercury Comet. I have a good husband.

–Marilyn Hurt

Grandma and the Girdle

My mother lived and worked in Vandalia, Illinois, a few hours south of me. Every year, she would use one of her vacation weeks to drive up for a visit with me and my family. Grandma (what I called Mom when my daughters were around) liked shopping. So at least once during our week, the four of us would load into the car and go to downtown Peoria where the merchandise was different from what was sold in Vandalia. This was before online shopping, or even shopping malls.

Grandma had been wanting a new girdle, and we found exactly what she had been looking for at Sears. The girls and I agreed to wait for her while she tried the girdle on.

"Grandma," I said. "Just give us a shout if you need any help."

We waited, and waited some more. Then came a weak cry for help. Grandma's voice, but nothing like we'd heard before, summoned the girls and me to the dressing room. There was the girdle— stretched and rolled like a rubber band, strangling Grandma at her mid-section. There were obvious signs of a struggle, most notably her mussed hair and beads of perspiration covering her face, but Grandma was laughing.

"I can't get it off!"

The fitting room was quite small, but Grandma invited us in to help. The task before us, urgent and clear, required all eight hands on Grandma and that girdle. We pulled on the girdle and stuffed parts of Grandma where they needed to go, stopping only for deep breaths and outbursts of uproarious laughter. Before we got that girdle off Grandma, we all had mussed hair and were moist with perspiration.

Grandma went to be with the Lord several years ago. My girls are grown and married with families of their own. We love getting together for shopping and other things, and when we do, funny things seem to happen. We'll always remember Grandma and the girdle. Thanks to Grandma, we know that one can't actually die from laughter. If that were possible, we all would have died that day, and Grandma would have had to meet Jesus wearing that girdle.

–JoAnn Brown

Through the Wringer

I ran my arm through the wringer of one of those old, backyard washing machines. Mom had stepped inside to answer the telephone, and I was her four-year-old helper. Doctors worked to straighten bones and save my arm. They watched in disbelief as full function returned to my arm, hand, and all five fingers involved. The scar at my left elbow serves to remind me of how God released me from that horrible pain and permanent disfigurement.

But my life really began when I was twenty-eight years old. My husband, Dan, and I were invited by neighbors to go to church. The people were kind and accepting. The Jesus I heard about was someone I needed. I wanted Him in my life. I believed and trusted Him with my future.

I was thirty-one before I trusted Him with my past.

One day, I packed what I planned to be the last lunch I'd make for Dan and delivered it to his place of work. Plans for a coward's way out had been formed and certain in my mind. Once I returned home, with a .22 caliber loaded, I contemplated the best placement of the muzzle. My finger was on the trigger.

The phone rang.

Calling about my son, the school secretary said, "He's not feeling well. You need to come and get him. He looks pretty miserable."

I laid down the gun and left to go pick up my youngest son from school.

Once he was home, comfortably medicated and falling asleep on the couch, I kissed his forehead and my thoughts returned to the gun. But having my child in the next room didn't seem right. The heavily wooded area behind our house would provide privacy.

I turned toward the door, holding the gun close to my body in such a way that, should my little boy wake up and follow me, he wouldn't see it. But my walk into the woods was interrupted. Chaotic thoughts bombarded my mind. New scenarios of being found conflicted with what I'd imagined during the previous week. None of them good. All of them involving my children being the first to discover the choice I'd made and left with a memory they'd never be able to erase.

Dan and I would soon be married for ten years, and if I was to live another week, I would have to tell him about the affair I had two years into our marriage. I was certain he would end our relationship and take my children if I told him. What would happen to the kids? Dan had already forgiven so much in our marriage relationship. The kids had already suffered enough because of me.

I kept our house like a morgue—doors, windows and curtains closed. I didn't want sunshine to expose me. When something terrible happened, and I knew it would, I didn't want the world to be watching. I feared and hated men. No man, including Dan, would be allowed to abuse or control me again. It's altogether possible that I feared and hated God for his strength and other traits I considered masculine.

Before I tell you much more, I want you to know that two years before he died, my dad (actually my step-dad) admitted he was a sinner who needed a savior. God did that; His timing and without my help. Dad tried to make amends, but he couldn't undo eighteen years of physical, mental and emotional abuse or cover my scars.

Shortly after seeing how Dad was changing, Mom said that she'd accepted Jesus as who the Bible says He is. She said she was in a good place spiritually. We had been estranged during most of my adult years. My own mother seemed content to not have me around, and frankly, the feeling was almost mutual. One Sunday, a particularly moving sermon caused me to call her and ask if she'd like to talk. She didn't refuse. Her response when I said something hinting of our past?

"Oh well. That was you."

Ours became a barely cordial relationship. She offered no friendship to my children. To them, she was a stranger they'd seen a few times.

Still, there had been no shortage of older women who loved and mentored me in the years since Dan and I married. They shared their past mistakes and constantly reminded me that God made us human on purpose. Dan's mom was a great teacher and model for me. Church ladies. I looked up to them, but never felt that I could be like them.

Dan, having a mother who loved, protected and accepted him, something I couldn't have, made me jealous. Many times I told my mother-in-law, "You could take a prostitute off the street and make her feel like part of your family!"

That wasn't stretching the truth, and it was something I could say without pointing a finger at myself. I'd been many other things in my life, but never that.

After Mom rejected my attempt to reconcile toward a meaningful relationship, I made an appointment to see a professional counselor. Those sessions helped to process and redirect some of my thoughts. My counselor urged me not to give what my parents had said about me (or to me) any space in my self-talk. That got easier, but the mirror seemed to talk back to me. "You won't amount to anything. You are good for nothing."

In the days after I put the gun away, I prayed for God to fix things. My prayers went nowhere. Or maybe God was saying, "No. Do it my way."

I couldn't eat or sleep. Telling Dan about the affair was one of two dreadful options. I couldn't rest and conceal my lie, and I couldn't live much longer with the shame. The image of that gun was still clear in my mind. I hadn't tried to wipe it away. I knew that as sure as Christ died to save me, there was a devil, and he wanted to destroy me. The voices in my mind got louder, and I felt as though God was avoiding me.

I had developed unhealthy coping mechanisms as a child. Between the ages of three and eleven, I would wind my hair tight around my right hand and pull hard enough that it left bald spots on my scalp. Simultaneously, I'd bite the two middle fingers of my left hand as hard as I could, until they bled. Then, I would hide the ugly skin in my mouth and suck my fingers in an attempt to soothe the pain. Now, as an adult, I'd used up all my coping tricks.

My husband was nothing like my step-dad who got more irritable, unpredictable, and angry as the day went on and with every drink. I'd learned how to deal with the hitting and getting knocked around. I got smarter, stronger and could run far and fast by the time I was eleven. Dan said he wanted only good for me, and he seemed to understand. But my parents had taught me how to hide and stay hidden, so that's what I'd been doing in my marriage.

I felt an urgency to tell Dan about the affair before both he and God gave up on me.

"I knew about the affair," Dan said. "I knew way back then. I just wanted you to be the one to tell me."

My secret was out, and my life had not crumbled around me, but the devil wasn't finished. Neither was God.

The next few days were somewhat of a blur. I do remember that Satan tried to say, "I told you so." Dan and I had no more secrets, and that felt good, but watching him deal with my confession and not knowing his thoughts was hard.

The night terrors that had started in my childhood were more frequent now. Dad always said I could "cuss like a sailor" and fight with the best of them, even in my sleep. I remember those dreams, vivid, detailed, and realistic. Someone was always chasing me, and one of us was getting killed. Just like when I was a kid, I'd wake up knowing I had dreamed, but still afraid. God hadn't fixed everything in our family just because I had confessed. Memories of my childhood crept in as I saw how my own children were reacting to me. Compared to what my parents had done, my own parenting failures seemed so minor. I'd resolved to never treat my kids the way my parents treated me. Holding to that low of a standard hurt all of us, even me.

When anything went wrong (and stuff happens in every family) I refused to accept responsibility. The kids and Dan were always blamed for my bad choices and behavior. I'd look at the eyes of my children and see myself at four, eight, or twelve years old. Then I'd get this feeling in my gut that my step-dad had been right. *Somebody should have knocked me in the head when I was born!*

I couldn't bring myself to change. I was stuck in a pattern that someone else had carved out for me. I counted on that old saying that "kids are resilient." My kids were every bit as resilient as I had been, maybe more, plus they were resourceful.

Abuse was familiar to me. You name it, I lived through it. Sexual, physical, verbal and emotional. My kids were repeating some my own coping behaviors, I'd been through that proverbial wringer and survived. It should have been easy for me to spot the signs in my own children, but I avoided looking. My childhood memories didn't resurface, as some people say theirs do. Mine had never quite been buried. When I worshipped or prayed, God made it clear that I needed to deal with my past, before I could move forward.

But like too many other little girls, I had more than one abuser. When I was three, an older (but still juvenile) family member began to touch me and tell me inappropriate secrets. That's about the time I created an alternative personality. Lisa grew up faster than me, but wasn't really much smarter. She exaggerated my confusion, and made sure I recalled specific days and hours and minutes.

I'd figured out how to pretend that it wasn't me in the room. I could be somewhere and someone else. Lisa was the one being hurt. She was a mean girl and knew how to fight back. I didn't like her, but I could tell her anything. She helped me to connive against both of my abusers. Lisa served a purpose, I suppose. She wasn't easy to be rid of. I finally had to outgrow her.

We had aunts and uncles who came to the house frequently. One of Dad's brothers confronted him about his drinking and the way he treated us, but nothing changed. Dad wouldn't visit with family after that.

Neighbors heard the yelling. When Dad got too loud, or started a rampage, they'd go inside and close the windows on our side of their house. I don't blame them. Who wouldn't be afraid of a man who'd been seen chasing his own family around the yard with a shovel or an ax?

Dad pulled out his shotgun more than once, and threatened. I don't know how our neighbors could not have heard.

While pulling weeds one summer as a young girl, I came into contact with poison ivy. The itching and swelling was bad enough, but I had trouble breathing and ended up in the emergency room. Medicine helped, but gave me hallucinations. Mom brought me home from the hospital, still very uncomfortable. It may have been because I was complaining, or it might have been the cost of my medical care that outraged him and caused Dad to drag me out of the house and throw me into the yard.

"You don't even know how to pull up weeds!"

I think the neighbors saw and heard.

I ran away from home several times. No one noticed much, and I generally came home within a few days. If I had known who my "real" dad was, I would have run to him, but Mom never would tell me his name, or even what town he was from. Lisa worked to convince me that he wouldn't be much of a father anyway, and I was better off without him.

If I couldn't hide, I lied. Whenever anyone saw a bruise or asked me how I was, my response was, "I'm fine." School teachers liked me. I was Mrs. Fane's Student of the Year. Mrs. Mitchell bought me lunch, and we ate together. I helped her grade papers and she gave me a cross necklace. I have other good childhood memories, but those two teachers were extra special.

My brothers punched holes in walls and my sister fought back. I kept trying to hide. Alcohol was available. I started using it for comfort. It made me feel as though I had control.

No one had given me "the talk" when I got my first boyfriend. Being sexually active at thirteen years old seemed to be my choice. My boyfriend didn't treat me right, but I didn't know what to expect from him. He's not to blame. I doubt anyone gave him a "talk" either.

Some of the things that had been said to me were fused to my self-image long before I met him. When my boyfriend was done with me, I was *"too fat and ugly to get a man."* I would *"never amount to anything."* I wasn't *"worth the powder to blow me to hell and back."* And there was always Dad's favorite, *"Somebody should have knocked you in the head when you were born!"*

I was used to being bullied. And I could take it. School was no picnic for kids from my "side of the tracks." That sounds old-fashioned and cliché, but a dumb set of railroad tracks still can separate the kids who have from the kids who don't.

So, in those days that followed my confession I decided that suicide, by gun or any other means, was not something I could do to my family. Without that option, I'd settle for being present, but not presentable.

But God wouldn't leave me alone or let me stay hidden.

One afternoon, I dropped to my knees over the grief I'd caused. I prayed and cried for what I know to be hours. God spoke to me, not in an audible way, but by reminding me of things I knew to be true.

I recalled and, in my mind, replayed the abuses and neglect of my childhood. Fantasies of revenge, and worse, were interrupted and erased as though my tears could wash them away. I had more to confess than the affair. The hatred and transferring of rage from my abusers to Dan and the kids pained me.

God didn't respond with the stern punishment I deserved. I'd been born again when I was twenty-eight. That afternoon, I learned to see God in a whole new way, like all five of my senses had been corrected. Christians talk about grace and mercy, and I had experienced both, but that day and the days after, grace and mercy flooded me.

Can God turn an eternal pessimist into an optimist? I think He did!

The colors of nature were brighter and bolder that day as I drove into town to do some mundane shopping. I'd been praying and thanking God during the entire trip. I headed home, and my car was full of evidence that I'd been to all my usual stores, but I couldn't have retraced my steps. I remembered none of the shopping. "For Pete's sake," I said to myself. "Surely my eyes were open!"

I was almost home when the vision of a little, blonde, curly-haired girl appeared in the street ahead of me. I knew she, and the man in the bright white robe who was holding her hand, were a vision, but I didn't want to blink and lose sight of them. There was no scar on the inside of her left elbow. I knew this was a God thing and I didn't want it to end, but tears caused the vision to leave me.

God has not revealed himself to me in that way since. I know if He sees that little girl without a scar on her left elbow, that He can see me now—healed and forgiven. Through the wringer? Yes. Physically, mentally, and emotionally? Yes.

Psalm 32:1-5 (NLT) has become one of my favorite passages of Scripture:

"Oh, what joy for those whose disobedience is forgiven, whose sin is put out of sight! Yes, what joy for those whose record the LORD has cleared of guilt, whose lives are lived in complete honesty! When I refused to confess my sin, my body wasted away, and I groaned all day long. Day and night your hand of discipline was heavy on me. My strength evaporated like water in the summer heat. Finally, I confessed all my sins to you and stopped trying to hide my guilt. I said to myself, 'I will confess my rebellion to the LORD.' And you forgave me! All my guilt is gone."

When I finally opened the curtains and windows of our family home, I saw the dirt, but I didn't see Dan in the same way. That we all needed to have some light in our lives was clear. I'm still apologizing for things I did and didn't do. I'm apologizing for things I don't remember doing or not doing.

But God has released me from "the wringer," and I'm not going there again.

On the other side of the wringer I am clean and new. I am loved, forgiven and accepted. I've no reason to run or to hide. Our marriage relationship was saved. Thank you, Jesus. Dan is the best! I give God all the credit, but Dan and I both deserve congratulations. We just celebrated our 35th wedding anniversary.

–Natalie Schnoor

I Like to Go to Church

I never thought about becoming a "church lady." I just became one. My mother and my mother's mother were church ladies, but it wasn't something I inherited or that came to me automatically. No one would have presumed this skinny, quiet, freckle-faced redhead to become much of anything, except I was a serious child, loved hearing stories about Jesus, and loved going to church.

At five years old, I was still calling her "Mommy" when my mother died, and soon after, my father married another church lady. My favorite aunts were church ladies, some less "churchy" than others. My favorite uncles were their counterparts, farmers and factory workers mostly.

Back in the late 1930s and 40s, if someone was sick or needed help in their home, it was usually a church lady who merged committee with compassion and got stuff done. If a cow got out of the pasture on a Sunday morning or a house caught fire, everyone knew you could have a healthy bunch of deacons running to your aid sooner than wake a hired professional. Those were some memorable times. I never wanted to miss a Sunday.

If anyone ever presumed me to turn into anything, I suppose it would have been the wife of a farmer or a factory worker. Those were the church men I admired most. But, for the longest time I wanted to be a missionary, and maybe go to China like the woman in one of my favorite stories. California would have been my second choice. But God would have to make it happen and I met Howard my senior year of high school.

One can never be certain if the thing they look back on was a detour of personal preference or God's chosen route all along. Howard, I came to believe, was both.

There isn't one specific pathway for becoming a church lady. I pretty much stuck to the route my parents set me on; not a lot of winding and turning or rest stops along the way. So now I'm in my eighties and not one for nostalgia, but my daughter had a moment of realizing she didn't know much about her mother's past. That's because yesterday holds either spilled milk kind of stories or vain glory thickened with afterthoughts. I'd rather talk about getting ready for tomorrow.

"What is it that you want to be known for?" she asked.

I'm sure she thought I would mention the raising of my four children. That would have been an easy answer, and I've got reason to brag. My job with the Illinois Department of Public Aid was important to me. My career provided a way to work out my Christian values and serve mankind (children and mothers more than men). God blessed my career many times over. Yet, when a stranger walks up to me and says, "Hey! I remember you," it's likely because of something I did as a church lady.

A couple of deacons from our church went to a conference and came home with a report about a new sort of ministry that was reaching a lot of children and families. I listened. These deacons were engineers both in their professions and personalities. They weren't known for jumping into anything without first measuring, planning and calculating. A touch of enthusiasm and a convincing argument caught Howard's and my attention. We were among the first to be recruited to work in the church's bus ministry. That was in the late sixties.

I was involved in a lot of church sponsored activities back then, but if I had to choose the one that made me a legitimate missionary without going to China or California, it would definitely be my work in the bus ministry. I've talked to several missionaries who've been to some amazing places and made a lot of disciples, but never met one who's been invited to step into a house or apartment and help a little boy find his boots so he could walk out in the snow, climb on a bus and go to church.

Please, don't get me wrong. I'd still hop on a plane or a boat to China if God wanted me to. Wouldn't that be something! And I've made it as far west as Los Angeles. A step-sister lived there, and that was a nice visit. Plenty of heathen live out in California, and Howard would have agreed to stay, but God didn't ask us to leave our home for more than a week, so we flew back to Illinois.

Fifty Saturdays, every year, for many years, I spent my mornings driving around and knocking on doors. My Saturday job as a bus "captain" was to remind kids and their parents to be watching for the big red, white and blue bus the next morning. I had to start early if I wanted to contact all the families and still make my regular hair appointment at 1 p.m. Lunch was often a sandwich on my way to the salon.

Fifty Sundays out of the year, I retraced my route from the day before, jumping down from the steps of a bus, walking or jogging up a sidewalk or through a muddy yard to knock on a door. I woke up a lot of parents, and they got used to ignoring me. Their children, however, didn't want to miss that bus. They loved going to church.

At 12:30 or 1 p.m. some of the moms and dads would greet us with a smile as the bus stopped in front of their home and returned their children. All too often, I knocked and there was no answer. I'd knock again, and there would be an apologetic glance between me and the child with the missing parent. Grocery shopping and hangover sleeping were generally the reason a "bus kid" would join me and my family for late noon meal. I learned to prepare for surprise guests when I bought a roast on Thursday night, or peeled potatoes and seasoned my green beans before leaving the house on Sunday mornings. My daughters had learned to pull together the Sunday dinner I'd started while they waited for me to finish the after-church bus route. Not once did Howard grumble about carrying an extra chair to our dining room table. A time or two (or four) a kid would let the other kids on the bus know about the meal they shared with our family. Then, over the next few weeks there would be a "rash" of absent parents after church on Sunday afternoons. Unless we had a commitment that afternoon, it wasn't a problem.

Don't think me a complainer. You don't do church lady work like that if it makes you miserable. I loved those kids. It was some of the parents who made me crazy. Funny thing: after lunch, I'd call the parent (no cell phones then), and let them know their child was safe. But rather than apologize and offer to come pick up their child, they would hesitate … until I offered to drive their kid, or kids, home.

Howard started out as a bus driver and maintenance/mechanic guy. His Saturday job, for most of those years, was to have five former school buses running and gassed up. His Sunday job was to show up, before the other bus drivers, and get those bus engines started. He loved the kids too, but at least once a year he would let me know I could quit. "It's your decision. You deserve a weekend just for you."

I had two weeks every year, away from both my work in the office and at church, a vacation to go and do whatever I chose. My children probably didn't suspect that our family vacations were as much about me getting away as they were about fun and creating fond family memories.

The years I served as a bus captain, and eventually as director of the ministry, were some of my best. Just the other day, a familiar looking little boy caught my eye. I would say he was about six years old. He was running circles around his mother who was trying to get her grocery shopping done. I smiled at him. He smiled back and took couple of steps in my direction. His mom grabbed his arm and reigned him in.

"He's fine," I said to her.

Then I got a look into the eyes of someone I knew from way back when. She rode my bus for several years. A quiet little girl with a pretty smile and a lot of trouble at home. She recognized me too.

"Your voice," she said. "It hasn't changed a bit. And you look the same."

Our eyes had aged over the same number of years since we'd seen each other, but her smile was just as pretty. She asked about Howard and my family. I asked about her. Life hadn't treated her too well. Some, because of bad choices put upon her by the adults in charge, and some, because she probably didn't see a way to make a better choice.

We could have talked much longer, but her little boy was restless to move on to the next aisle. "Stop by the house some time," I said. "Howard would love to see you."

"I will."

"Do you remember the address?"

"Oh yeah. I remember. I had lunch there a couple times."

"Of course you did!"

"Mrs. Lisanby," she said. "Those were some good times."

She stooped down and turned the shoulders of her son so he faced her.

"Wesley, do you remember the song I sing whenever I see a bus?"

Evidently he did, because he jumped right into the chorus and sang, "The wheels on the bus go round and round. Round and round. Round and round. The wheels on the bus go round and round, all through the town."

"This is the lady who used to take me to church on the bus," she told him.

But Wesley was not impressed, nor did he stop tugging on his mother's blouse, urging her to keep moving toward the cereal aisle. We started to push our carts in opposite directions, and then she turned and reached for a hug.

I'd come to the grocery store for a few fast-lane items, and left with more of a roast than Howard and I needed for our Sunday dinner. I hoped to see Wesley and his mother again. I'm forever a church lady, and I never want to miss a Sunday.

–Ellene Lisanby
1931-2017
(Ellene's story is based on personal interview and supported by entries in her journal.)

The Children's Home

Sissy held tight to Cora Lee's hand,
Tears rolling down her face,
"Why can't I go with you, Mommy?
I don't want to stay in this place."
She pleaded with her tearful mom.
"I'll be good. You know I will
Not be a bother to anyone.
Let me go with you and Bill."
A lady slowly walked toward them
In a long black dress and weird hat.
Her skirt swished as she drew nearer.
Sissy whispered, "Mom, who is that?"
She's called a nun, or a sister," Cora said.
"And she will take good care of you,
As long as you are sweet and willing
To do what she tells you to!
Now you be a big, brave girl, Sissy.
I've got important things to do.
I promise it won't be very long

'Til I come back for you."
Sissy's short legs tried hard to keep up
As she walked with the nun down the hall.
Looking back to see if her mom had left,
She spied a figure hanging on the wall.
The man was looking down at her from a cross.
Sissy thought, Lola's told me about Him.
He had to die to save the world
From the devil and all our sin.
There was a wreath of thorns upon His head
And blood ran down His face and hair,
But His eyes told Sissy that he sympathized
Because He didn't want to be up there!
It was years before I realized how this encounter with God's perfect Son
Mapped out the route that I must take in running the race I run.

–Anita Allen

For the Record

I'm compelled to put this on paper and get it out of my way.
This heart of mine holds no grudge, just regrets from yesterday.
A man entered my world in '44, bringing hopes of family stability.
Though I knew he wasn't my father, I really wanted him to be.
He accepted me as his daughter the day he married Cora Lee.
Their marriage grew quite stormy as the hands of time ticked by.
Many nights I'd listen to the warring couple and sleep in the tears I'd cried.
By the time I approached my teenaged years, I'd grown accustomed to their fights,
And came to the childlike conclusion that the barks were worse than their bites.
Usually my mind took my stepdad's side, for he was always so good to me.
I was grateful for his efforts in providing for our family.
Rarely did he ever complain, and money was always tight.
Seldom in my mother's eyes did he ever do anything right.
I guess I'm writing all this down to show the love and trust we shared.
Of all the people, in all the world, I thought he loved me and really cared.

One night when Mom was working, third shift, in an all-night café
Fear replaced trust and respect, but the love never went away.
[A portion of this poem is deliberately omitted.]
For weeks I wondered what to do. I didn't want to create a row.
My heart said to tell my mother, but it didn't tell me how.
Opportunity arose one afternoon, when Bill was out of town.
"There's something I have to tell you, Mom. But first you'd better sit down.
You must promise me and swear, Mother, to think before you act.
My intentions are for you to do nothing, but be aware of the disturbing facts."
I could tell as she began to speak, her promise now meant nil.
Leaving in hurt and anger for Gulf State's Truckyard to await the return of Bill.
I've never told this to anyone. It's been painful as a dart.
In order to dwell on better things, I just had to bare my heart.
Many times I wanted to tell Russel, but the words could not be spoken.
I forgave my stepdad long ago, but my heart remains still broken.
In this age of promiscuity, this happening doesn't sound so bad.
Except for the destruction of faith and trust, I once held for my stepdad.
Years have passed, and I love the man for the many good things he did.
Aside from this act, I can honestly say, he always treated me as his own kid.
At the start I said, I hold no grudge, only regret from yesterday.
Thank God it's now on record and finally out of my way.

–Anita Allen

The Hardest Pain

It's 3:00 a.m. I haven't slept. My burdens are as lead.
Fumbling for my glasses, I quietly get out of bed
And make my way through the darkness 'til my fingers find the light.
And I say aloud to the silent room, "My God, I hurt tonight."
My concerns are for my husband, Russ. "You know he's very ill.
He needs more than a magic elixir or a powerful prescription pill.
Let him touch the hem of your garment to physically be made whole.
If it's not your will to heal him, Lord, please save his precious soul.
In all our years together, he's never done anything bad.
He's been my faithful husband and a wonderful, caring dad.
If there's any flaw in his character, it's the stubbornness of his will.
But in my heart, somehow I know, Russ is aware you love him still."
Reaching for my Bible to delve into The Word,
Tears fell on the pages, causing all to blur.
I cannot read, so best I pray, then I felt the Spirit stir.
He said, "I am your Comforter from God on High
To assure you that the soul you love will never ever die.
Through Jesus Christ, your prayers are heard by a loving compassionate ear.
And knowing your faith in eternity, He will hold your husband near."

[Few of us pray with perfect theology in mind all the time, but God knows our hearts. Days before he passed away, Russ finally professed his need for a Savior and faith in Jesus Christ, aloud. I sure loved that stubborn man.]

–Anita Allen

Goodbye, Blue Hat

Christmas Day 1950 was the date we set for our wedding. F.M. (Red) and I were both teachers and had two weeks of vacation time at Christmas. It seemed like a good idea. We could have the wedding at the beginning of the week and still have a few days for a short trip to New Orleans.

Red's brother, being a minister, would be in Tennessee visiting family over the holidays, and he was more than happy to perform our wedding ceremony. We made these plans in September, so right away, I needed to decide what to wear!

I had my wedding dress, but doesn't every bride need a going-away outfit?

A friend, who taught home economics in the same school where I taught English, volunteered to make an outfit for me. She helped me shop for a pattern—a two-piece suit, and then we spotted the fabric. A beautiful blue velvet!

It occurred to me that such a suit should have a matching hat, but finding the right one proved to be difficult. If a hat was the right color, it was an awful style, or had no style at all. That beautiful, blue suit demanded "suitable" accessories! Fortunately, another of my friends knew of a lady known for making beautiful hats, and this lady lived conveniently on the outskirts of town. I paid her a visit and learned that she would indeed make a hat for me if I brought her some of the material. Plus, I could have it in plenty of time for my big day.

Our wedding took place at four o'clock on Christmas Day, so by the time all the traditional wedding proceedings were complete, it was getting late and we needed to be on our way.

I changed from my wedding dress into my beautiful blue velvet suit and my blue velvet hat, which by the way, had a turned up, half brim that was generously embellished with rhinestones. We drove away from my parent's home in our 1949 Chevrolet, on our way to New Orleans!

We were driving merrily along, having just come through the business district of the small town of Henderson, Tennessee when a car zoomed past us. Its passengers gestured wildly and yelled words we couldn't understand at first. We finally understood they were trying to let us know we had a flat tire or very nearly flat tire!

Having dampened our spirits with that bit of news, they went on their way while we pulled over to the side and pondered the situation. Neither of us wanted to spend the evening of our wedding, or our first Christmas as man and wife, changing a dirty car tire. Neither of us was dressed for the task. Red suddenly remembered having noticed a service station, just a few blocks back. We'd turn the car around and head to that station to get the tire repaired.

It proved to be just a neighborhood station with a couple of gas pumps, but yes, they could take care of our tire problem. We breathed a sigh of relief and shared a moment of silence. Then, simultaneously, we realized a small hamburger joint was attached to the service station. It was well past dusk, and we had some distance to go before our final stop of the night. Red suggested we go in that little cafe and have something to eat while we waited. Not that either of us was hungry, but we did need a place to wait.

It seemed clean and bright but only two customers were there, sitting at the small counter. Red and I chose one of the two booths near the door. The other two customers were teenage girls, wearing blue jeans with cuffs turned up, saddle oxfords and plaid shirts with the tails out. Not exactly Christmas day apparel! Red wore one of his school-teacher suits, and there I was with my beautifully tailored, blue velvet suit and my matching hat, complete with rhinestones.

We ordered our food, and were beginning to relax a bit in spite of our circumstances, when the girls left the counter. They strolled across the room and left through the door which was directly behind us. The door burst open, which got our attention. Then, one of the girls stuck her head back in as she loudly and mockingly said, "Goodbye, Blue Hat!"

It may have been a beautiful hat, but my love for it faded after having that flat tire.

–Aletha Oakley

Love is Never Late

I was the newbie sitting around a table of women who had known each other for a while when one of them asked me how long I'd been married. I was in my mid-fifties at the time and these older women had been married a while, so they might have expected me to say something like twenty years.

"Almost two years," I replied with a smile.

First were looks of surprise followed by expressions of delight and comments like, "You're still a newlywed!" Then came the inevitable question, "Tell us how you met your husband."

I chuckled to myself, took a sip of water, and gathered my thoughts. I briefly thought about my nearly non-existent love life. If I hadn't stepped out of my comfort zone, I would not be sitting here at all.

I decided to give the short answer to their question. "We met on eharmony." More gasps of delight preceded comments from a few ladies who had known some others who met their spouses that way. The conversation quickly drifted away from me, but my thoughts lingered on the longer story.

Always a bit of an introvert, I had been perfectly content living alone. When I needed social time, I hung out with family. That routine suited me just fine—for a while. I had moments of longing for love and companionship. Every once in a while I met a man who caught my interest, but feelings usually ended up being one-sided and nothing ever worked out.

Once I hit my forties, I started thinking more about my future. I mean, having a cat is great and all, but just try getting one to help you make big decisions or fix a car! It was about that time when internet dating started to gain a little credibility. I checked it out on one of those free trials and realized I wasn't quite ready for that. I wanted to meet someone the old-fashioned way.

Meanwhile, I used my free time to socialize more with friends—get out of the house a bit more—and get to know myself better. Toward the end of my fourth decade of life I was finally ready to make some changes.

The turning point came at a time after I'd gone through some major life changes. I left a job I'd been at for fifteen years, I started a new job, and had two cars rear-ended and totaled within a month of each other. I was stressed and emotionally spent by the end of that year. I had a wonderful support system of friends and family in place, but coming home to a cat just wasn't cutting it anymore. I longed to come home to someone. *Is it too late?*

Since I wasn't meeting any men through work or church, I decided once more to try internet dating. I wish that I could say that I found the love of my life quickly, but I did not. I met all kinds of men and had a few relationships, but nothing stuck. A couple of experiences left me emotionally spent, so I put dating on hold. The process took a few years, but during that time I grew spiritually and emotionally. I became a voracious reader of nonfiction books in the spiritual and relationship genres. I also sought out married mentors who listened to and encouraged me.

Feeling stronger after a three-year hiatus from dating, I jumped back into internet dating and met someone. That relationship lasted much longer than all the others, but ended when we had different ideas about our futures.

Though I still felt some pain from the last relationship breakup, I decided to try internet dating one more time. At that point in my life, I thought I would settle for just making some new friends and decided I shouldn't get serious about anyone. After all, the scars from the last relationship were still in the final stages of healing and I had to protect my heart. *Okay, I'll just do this for fun.*

A few weeks into online dating, I noticed that sometimes men would review my profile, but leave without ever saying anything. If they lived in other states or their profiles didn't interest me, I just shrugged and moved on. However, one man who viewed my profile lived just a few short minutes from my home. It's unusual to find someone who lived so close, and curiosity caused me to scrutinize his profile. *Hmmm.* I noticed immediately we had a common interest in singing. I pondered this for a moment, but decided that if he was interested he would have initiated a conversation. *He's not interested.*

The next morning, I thought again about Neil, the internet stranger who likes to sing, and I decided to do something about it—about this guy, Neil. I opened my computer, viewed his profile, and lingered a moment before sending him a smile. That same evening, he responded with a brief and friendly message. We continued to correspond for a few days, then graduated to talking on the telephone. Within a few weeks we met in person for dinner at a restaurant.

You might be thinking that was the beginning of love, and in a way it was. But I like to think of it as the framework for what became love. You can't build a house without a strong foundation and sturdy framework. I was still working through feelings from my previous relationship and didn't plan on getting serious with anyone right away. After a few dates, my future husband and I had a heart-to-heart talk. He helped me realize that I needed to make up my mind about what I wanted. I needed to take some time to decide this before jumping into another relationship, and I didn't want to string him along. His gentleness, thoughtfulness, and understanding impressed me deeply. It was the spark of something.

I took the time I needed to let my heart heal, reflect on my life, and look toward the future. No dating. No correspondence or phone calls with men.

At the end of two months and a lot of soul-searching, I was finally free from the weight of the past. I felt able to embrace a future that was different from the one I had imagined a year before. I messaged my new friend to see if he was still interested and available. We began dating again and married a year later.

Now, as the party was coming to an end and women were gathering their leftovers from the potluck, Neil came over and asked if I was ready to go home. After reminiscing about our history together this evening, I realized that love is never late. I smiled, knowing I had someone to go home with and said, "Yes, let's go home."

–Kristi West Breeden

His Strength. His Time. My People

Musicians played horns, saxophones, flutes, and other instruments. It would have been loud, even without the organ and a congregation of people singing, clapping, and stomping their feet. Hands were waving, and people were falling to and rolling on the floor. When the music paused, the random shouting kept the tension building.

No, this wasn't my first rock concert! My mother had insisted our family return to her people and to her church.

I was bewildered, scared and twelve years old. I began to shake and cry. Mom pretended not to notice. It was hard to sense what Dad was thinking. His facial expression was as new to me as the response of the congregation to, "Let's stand and praise God!"

My older sister, Deborah, seemed to be somewhere between overwhelmed and entertained. I was never more uncomfortable than in that moment, and I wanted to leave.

What happened next was the most frightening thing I had ever experienced. Two of the "church ladies" came over to me, each grabbing an arm and claiming an ear to yell into. They dragged me toward the front of the room, trying to explain that I needed to go to the altar so that "Brother So and So" could lay hands on me and pray. They yelled loud enough for everyone in the near vicinity to hear how I was "lost," and that I needed "The Holy Ghost."

I didn't know what Mom had told these ladies about me, or if she had told them anything at all, but I had already decided to follow Jesus. It hadn't been that long ago. While at a Christian summer camp, I had felt what I believed to be the Holy Spirit prompting me to trust Him. A counselor had prayed with me.

Our family had been in church (a good church), and I had been in Sunday school since I was a baby. As a pre-teen, I had much to learn, but I knew the Bible stories, and was old enough to understand what I was doing. I wanted to be a Christian. Jesus had always been a part of my life, but I decided to trust Him with my life at Camp Good News. I asked Mom if I could be baptized at camp. She said, "No!"

With these two women in control of my body, and my parents allowing it, I doubted. I knew my soul was no longer lost. I felt sure that I was a child of God. These people made me think I must be missing something, but I wasn't convinced enough that I would have taken a step toward that altar without their aggression.

I have never spoken a language I didn't understand, and the Holy Spirit had never caused me to fall to the ground and shout. Still, they assumed a lot from my trembling body and my tears. I never did figure out why it was me, and not Deborah, who got dragged to the altar, but sometimes I wondered if it had something to do with Mom thinking that my camp experience with Jesus was not enough.

I remember the argument between my parents about going back to Indiana, not to live, but once a week for church. Mom won, the way she always did—with blaming and threats. Dad did a lot to appease her. Traveling to Terre Haute, a three-and-one-half-hour drive, just so Mom could say she had been to church was only one of the ways Dad yielded control to her.

I wanted to scream. We had loads of churches in town. *Why isn't one of them good enough?* The argument ended when, to make Mom happy, and for the sake of peace, Dad agreed to take us to Terre Haute.

Mom hadn't told us much about her early years. Dad, a Peoria, Illinois native, met Mom in Vincennes, Indiana. They were married in Vincennes and then came to Peoria, I suspect for two reasons; one being Dad's employment, and the other being to escape the meddling and control of Mom's people.

Dad's family had attended Methodist, Presbyterian and Baptist churches. After Deborah and I were born, we went, too. We attended a Christian school for a while, but Mom was not comfortable with any church or school Dad chose, and she made it known.

It was hot and humid that first day we drove to Indiana for church. Mom put on a sleeveless dress and complained that she would be hot with the matching jacket on.

Dad said, "It's a nice dress. You look fine without the jacket."

"Oh no," Mom insisted. "My arms need to be covered when I'm in *my* church. I have to wear the jacket!"

Deborah and I thought it strange that the church service was on a Saturday night, and that we were expected to attend again late Sunday afternoon. That's an awful lot of singing and shouting. Even the minister shouted when it didn't seem necessary. I hoped Mom had had her fill.

During our long ride home Dad gave Mom plenty of opportunity to change her mind and admit that returning to her past had been a bad idea. We listened as she defended her decision and the ways of her people. Why Mom was so desperate to oblige these strangers remained a mystery to me. But she made it very clear that I was to fit in, too.

Mom's bad idea was made worse because our family had to spend the night with her people. "Church people." Sometimes we stayed in hotel-like rooms, located in the basement of the church. Weird and creepy. We could never miss a service!

Later, our family started traveling, every other weekend, to another arm of the same church in Moline, Illinois. That was only two hours away, but not much else was different.

On the first Monday after meeting Mom's people, I had a pair of pants that was already too short for me and was preparing to cut off the legs and make myself a pair of shorts. Mom walked into the room and asked what I was doing. I told her. She proceeded to tell me there would be no more shorts, slacks, jeans or anything of that nature, now that I had been to the altar.

"What do you mean? Why?" I asked.

My question angered her. She picked up the scissors and clenched them in a tight fist. The point was within inches of my throat.

"You'll do what I say. I'll tell you what you can and can't do or I'll just kill you!"

I cowered at her feet. The two most frightening things that have ever happened to me happened a day apart, and because of my mother. I knew my life had changed, and dramatically. I almost wished my life had ended. I'd just begun the seventh grade, and should have been excited. Being handed a whole new set of lifestyle rules, eighty-two in total, as a seventh grader, well … it was horrible!

The rule that, on the surface, seemed to impact my life most severely was that rule about how a woman should appear and dress. A woman's hair must not be cut, a woman must not wear men's clothing (no pants or shorts) and a woman must not show off her body in any way that could cause a man to sin. Long hair was to be worn up, preferably on top of the head. Dresses and skirts were always below the knee, but no farther.

Rules, rules and always more rules! Here is a sample:

- "You should never have a different judgment on any issue than the pastor. You should know your pastor's attitudes and methods of working, and then support them." (Rule #29 of 82).
- "Never challenge the authority, knowledge, or experience of the pastor. The Lord will take care of any deficiency on the part of the minister." (Rule # 36 of 82).
- The pastor's personal favorite was, "Don't try to second guess what the pastor means by what he says, an expression on his face, or an action because you could be wrong." (Rule # 61 of 82).

Television and movies were for sinners. Giving 10% of our income was expected, but to be a leader or a member in good standing, you needed to give more. Church members could not date or marry outside the church. Even then, the pastor must approve. We were supposed to ask permission of the pastor before leaving town for a vacation or buying a different automobile. Having his approval was the most important goal for our families, or at least the parents.

I made friends whose mothers or fathers were as adamant about pleasing the pastor as my mom was. We commiserated, but never too loudly. Rules about how women had no voice or authority in the church baffled us because mine wasn't the only mother who ruled with a heavy hand at home, but passively accepted a silent role around church people.

Having friends and socializing outside the church was forbidden. Because we lived so far away and rotated churches every other week, mine was a lonely existence.

When I did make friends with a girl at school, who happened to attend a Pentecostal church, I cautiously told Mom about her and asked permission.

Forty-eight years later, Mary and I are still best friends because, at least one time, Mom compromised for me. I thank God for bringing Mary into my life at such a critical time.

Once in a while, I was allowed to go with Mary to her church youth activities. The stark difference in our circumstances (primarily our churches) made me long to grow up and make my own choices. Mom's church tried to tell me that anyone who didn't belong to their specific group was going to hell. When I couldn't tune out the lies, I talked back under my breath, but fiercely.

Mom was thrilled by the prospect of my being baptized. But her thrill turned to disappointment and shame when I came out of the water without what was taught to be evidence of being a true "Holy Ghost Christian." I didn't "arise from the water speaking in tongues." She told me (verbally) that I wasn't wanted. Plus, I sensed the great deal of the shame her people dumped on her because of me.

I simply could not feel what those people told me I ought to feel. I worshiped God with them, and enjoyed some aspects of their community, but I didn't fit in, and didn't care to fake it. Yet, I was bound to them and their rules along with my mother. Dad, Deborah and I were all stifled, and waiting for the right time to break loose.

People might want to argue about whether Mom's "church" was a cult or not. I added up the clues and figured out the truth in a short amount of time. They wrongly siphoned glory and authority from Scripture and poured it over a man…a false teacher, a wolf in sheep's clothing and someone other than Jesus. Pardon for sin and grace for the helpless was awarded in exchange for loyalty. Nothing from that cult was offered freely. We all saw evidence manipulated and witnesses silenced. Why my mother would return, and take us with her to the prison from which she had been released is beyond my comprehension. Like many of the youth involved, I was serving my time and biting my tongue.

I was extremely depressed upon entering high school. Lots of kids were different, but to me, they were different because they chose to be. Deborah had somehow avoided the chains of Mom's church. Within reason, she could wear a normal hairstyle and stylish clothes. I assumed it was because she was older and most certainly would have caused a bigger, more embarrassing rebellion than I was willing to risk.

On the way to our lockers one day, I heard the conversation going on in front of me. My sister and her friend did not realize I was there.

"Debbie, I heard that weird girl with the long hair and long dresses is your sister."

Deborah's response was, "Oh, no, I don't know where you heard that from, but no, she's not!"

My heart sank to my gut as I opened my locker, exchanged one book for another and then slammed metal against metal. My devastation went unnoticed.

By the time I was sixteen, I decided to be done with all the rules. I drove to the mall, where I bought myself an outfit. Driving was a privilege, but the mall was crossing a line. *A short sleeved top and slacks is a brave place to start.* It was a brave move for me, but brave at the mall and brave at home were not the same kind of brave. My sister had moved out of the house by then, so I drove to her place, and changed into my new outfit.

She was amazed and pleased with my decision. We agreed, since she got along with Mom far better than I ever did, that we should drive to our parents' house together, but she would go in before me to announce my decision. Deborah came back outside wearing that bad-news face.

Mom had instructed her to tell me I was "… no longer her daughter."

God alone knows what my dad had to say, if anything.

Life isn't easy for a teen girl when she's living on her own and trying to finish high school. I lived in different places with relatives, friends, at the YWCA, or anyplace other than my parents' house.

I had hopes of enrolling at Bradley University and studying to become a nurse. Dad had worked in various departments and positions at Bradley, and was teaching the obscure subject of horology (the study of watchmaking). My tuition at Bradley would have been waived.

Although I wasn't living with my parents, I went back and forth some. Things were cold, but cordial. As long as I could make my own choices, I decided to go on a date, a blind date, with a guy who didn't go to church, any church. He was so thoughtful, and good to me. Dad thought he was a "stand-up guy." You guessed it, Mom didn't care for him at all.

The pressure between staying in school and getting a job to support myself wouldn't let up. High school was about to lose the battle, but Don, the blind date guy, insisted.

"You've got to stay in school. You've got to graduate. If you don't, it'll be the biggest regret of your life."

I knew he was right. I went to school half days, and worked as many hours as I could in a discount department store.

Mom decided it was time to move back to Indiana. She'd be closer to her people, which meant her church and a few of her relatives. My opportunity for a college education instantly vanished because Dad was no longer an instructor at the University.

Later on, I learned from Mom's younger brother how this had caused my dad much sorrow. My uncle reported about how Dad had wept and poured out his feelings, that he'd wanted nothing to do with mom's people and he knew she was caught up in a wicked mess. But Dad had no power to change Mom's heart or mind.

I remember that same uncle asking my mom, "If Brother So and So told you to go jump off a bridge, would you do it?"

"Yes, I probably would."

His name doesn't matter. The leader of this cult had fooled hundreds, if not thousands, of people to settle for his approval and give him control of their privilege as Christians; and Christians is what they claimed to be. They sacrificed a life of abundance in Christ Jesus for one man's lies.

The pastor was eventually arrested and charged with a few of his numerous sexual abuses. Due to the man's age and ill health at the time of his conviction, a lenient judge sentenced him to five years of probation and ordered him restricted from the church, children, and teenagers. He died, having destroyed many families. When his "church" was disbanded, other men took advantage of the void he'd created.

I'd been right to feel wary of this man and his church, but despite the facts, Mom remained loyal to the man's status and reputation. I've questioned God many times. "Why me?" "Why my family?" "Why my mother?" I would say, "Life could have been so much better."

But why is no longer important.

Two terrible days turned my life upside-down. Other days sent me spiraling downward. One blind date…and my life seemed to flip right-side up again. Not that life got easy or perfect. Not even that I gained control.

My husband, Don, was not a church-going believer, and although I longed to return to a place of community worship, I feared whatever it was that had trapped and wounded my mom. Don helped me finish and graduate from high school. I will forever be thankful for this. We agreed that it would be good for our girls to grow up in a Bible-believing, non-cult church. He was a truck driver and was gone a lot. The girls and I went to church without him. I didn't pressure him the way my mother would have.

When our oldest daughter was about to be baptized, I explained just a little of my past and my first baptism to our pastor and asked if I could be baptized again. He didn't think it was necessary, but agreed to an expression of my true and public commitment to Christ.

What a blessed day!

Years later, Don started listening to Christian radio when he was on the road. He came in the door looking different and with a new attitude one day. God had been teaching and leading him for weeks and I hadn't known about it. (Honestly, if I had, I might have nagged and ruined things by trying to hurry God along.)

God is good, and more patient than I'll ever be!

When we started attending a different church, closer to our home, the subject of baptism came up. That pastor said we would need to be baptized again, if we wanted to be members there. Old haunts rose within me, and I couldn't go to that church, or any church for a while. With no one to encourage me, it was easy to stay home on Sundays. Don was still driving a truck and doing most of his worshipping along with the radio.

I came home from work on December 28, 2016 to find Don unresponsive. They couldn't revive him. Thirty-eight years of marriage, two daughters, three grandchildren later, and he was gone.

We hadn't attended church in a very long while. I knew I was as vulnerable as ever without Don, and my history with church left me feeling alone and sort of helpless. Certainly, indecisive. So I prayed.

My daughter, Jennifer, said, "Liberty Baptist has a new pastor. I hear he's great."

"Who told you that?"

"My friend, Angie."

"You go," I said. "I don't think I'm ready."

Jennifer offered an extra dose of support, "I'll go with you."

"Okay. Fine."

But something came up and Jennifer wasn't able to make it. I wanted to back out. Fearful and nervous … but church, here I come! With every step, I was tempted to turn and run back to my car.

An older couple greeted me at the entrance. He told me to call him Red, and he wore a suit. Her name was Aletha, and she wore a dress. She also wore lipstick and had a short hairstyle. I was glad. Red's soft-spoken and friendly voice reminded me of my Dad, and they looked somewhat alike. As I walked into the sanctuary, more people welcomed me.

I intentionally chose to sit on the end of a pew and toward the back. My departure would not interrupt anyone's worship and would not take long!

A welcome pamphlet gave me something to fidget with and read while I waited for things to get started. Bible study, taught by members other than the pastor. *That is good.* Ways for kids and teens to stay out of trouble. *That's great.*

A faith-based cancer support group? *That's different.*

Tears of joy began to fall down my face as I looked up in prayer, "Well God, I guess this is where you want me to be!"

Don had died exactly six months before this day. And, only one month earlier, I had been diagnosed with chronic lymphocytic leukemia.

I met Venita, the lady who started the cancer support ministry, and her husband Gary. As I left the building, and even after I was home, I knew I had stepped into the exact place where God wanted me to be. Indescribable!

In one of his sermons the pastor said, "Don't go by what I say, look it up in God's Word for yourself." *Now that is an interesting challenge.*

Within a couple of weeks, I was a member of a Sunday school class and going on Wednesday evenings. Everyone is invited for the meal, and that is one night of the week I don't have to cook or eat alone. I can ask questions, get answers, and not be judged.

Little confirmations and encouragements tell me all the time, "You're in a good place." Then there are the bigger reminders; like my granddaughter, Juliet, becoming a Christian and being baptized.

Something far beyond what I could ever have imagined is about to happen. In a very short time, I will be facilitating our church's first official grief support group. God urged me, and is now giving me strength. God's timing is perfect and protective. He stayed with me when I was broken and alone. God actually planned for me. He knew me before he planted me in my mother's womb. He wanted me, and He used my journey to prepare me.

And now, I have a wonderful, loving church family, and am glad to say, "I found my people."

–Dalene Stewart

An Encounter with God

It was one of those moments, straight out of a movie. You know the one. The background noise fades away and everything except the main character goes out of focus.

Several days before, a girl in my third grade class told me she prayed every night for God to save her. I asked her to explain, and she told me she had asked God to take out her old, sinful heart and give her a new, clean one. I found this confusing, so I started asking questions at home.

Mom and Dad answered my questions to the best of their ability. My family had been going to church, off and on, since I was an infant. I had heard most of the Bible stories told in Sunday school. However, knowledge doesn't equal understanding. Fortunately, God's timing is perfect. Dad took me to a couple of special worship services that week. They called them "revival" meetings. By Sunday morning, I was beginning to have a sense of what God wanted from me.

The "movie moment" happened as I sat in my Sunday school class. As the teacher talked and children were answering, I heard and saw none of it. In my own private world, my mind was occupied with everything I'd learned that week. I mulled over this recent information until there was clarity. I had a choice to make. *Do I want to truly follow Jesus or just go to church?*

I decided, yes. I wanted to completely belong to God. I made that choice in my heart and nodded my head. I think I even said the word "yes" out loud. Immediately, the people around me came into focus and their sounds filled the room.

I felt impatient to get upstairs for the sermon because I knew there would be an opportunity for me to announce my decision. A lot of people came to church that morning, and we found ourselves sitting in the middle of a full pew. I listened carefully to every word the preacher said, while anxiously waiting for the sermon to end.

The opportunity finally came and we all stood to sing a song, but I was trapped. I looked both ways to the ends of the pew, but couldn't see how to get past all of the people. I needed to get to the front so I could talk to the preacher.

I began to feel panic until I noticed the pew seat, made vacant now that we were standing. I climbed onto the pew, and then crawled on my hands and knees until I got to the end of the pew. There I faced another challenge. The old-fashioned pews had tall ends. Having come this far, however, I was determined to get out. I stood and climbed over the end. As soon as my feet were on the floor, and I turned to walk toward the front of the church, tears began streaming down my face.

Not a child who cried easily, I was unprepared for the overwhelming emotion. By the time I got to the front, I could barely speak through the sobs. I hardly heard what the preacher said as we knelt to pray. I only knew I had encountered the real and living God.

–Kathy Stanford

The Fire

If I could cross every finger and toe on my body, I was doing it as I checked Tessa's head that morning. After five days of a fever with my five-year-old, I was done. As a mama, there's this fine line between sensitive caregiver and "for the love of the Sweet Lord above. Go. Back. To. School!" I was right in the middle … no, that's a lie. I was edging more toward the "Sweet Lord" side.

Ninety-eight point four degrees. I checked the thermometer again. Yes, 98.4°! I did a happy dance.

"You're good!" Go pick out some clean clothes," I said, and then sent her to the mountain of clean laundry on the couch. "Get ready to catch the bus."

Ruthie and Tessa launched out the door and up into the school bus. Joanna grabbed a bag of mini muffins and her blanky and headed to the chair in the living room. I interpreted her two-year-old language, opened the pouch of muffins and flipped on *Chip and Potato*. Thanks, Netflix.

My coffee needed a reheat, and I scarfed down a bowl of Lucky Charms. I jumped on Instagram real quick and recorded a few stories about the plan for the day. My mother-in-law, Pam, and I were excited about doing the last little bit of painting at our animal feed store, which was turning into a human feed store now that half of the space was a restaurant. We named it "The Feed Store." Not confusing at all!

I carefully considered just how much detail was necessary in my sharing of "The Wineinger House Survived the Flu" story. One of two adults and two of three children, the last of us recovered on this date. Twenty minutes passed. Joanna and I headed out for the day. I dropped her at daycare and drove to work.

It was refreshing to get back into my office. It felt like I hadn't been there for, well, five days! Emails … phone calls … chick orders … bills! My to-do list was long and urgent. I was also "running" the counter that morning. Technically, I was walking laps from my office to the register. I love my job.

I called to chat with the school nurse around eleven o'clock. She'd check with the teacher, but Tess was doing great. The door dinger chimed, so I'm off to the races again.

On my way, Pam called out, "Last wall!"

Painting was almost done. Hallelujah! Roger, our local auto mechanic and loyal chicken customer was on his lunch break getting some feed for his hens. We chatted about the ten inches of snow forecasted for that afternoon. Ugh. More snow, and a lot of it.

Roger walked out to load up his truck. I heard a fan. *That's a really loud fan!* Pam must have turned it on to dry the paint, or so I thought.

Roger poked his head back inside, "Something's not right."

Pam started shouting from the back, "What is that? I think it's coming from the warehouse…"

Still yelling, she attempted to open the walk-through door. It wasn't budging. I rushed outside, past Roger's truck, to see black and orange, but it wasn't registering. Fire flashed through a blown-out warehouse window.

"Lindsay! Move! Go. Move!"

I bolted back to the door and when I stepped in, Pam yelled, "Get out! Someone call 911! It's a FIRE! A FIRE!"

Black smoke billowed in from around the stuck door and the loading pull-up door—fast. Having been taught not to go back into a burning building for anything that isn't breathing, I ran to the back and grabbed my phone before running outside. Town sirens were already blaring.

My internal voice screamed, "Move the cars!"

I jumped immediately into my van, parked next to the building, and drove it across the street and out of the way. Then, back to rescue the other car, driving and dialing. *Nathan, pick up. Pick up.*

As soon as I heard my husband's voice, "The store is on fire!"

Business owners and locals were coming out as I stepped out of the car and onto the parking lot across the street. Ruth was one of them. When I saw her running in my direction, it hit me. I turned and looked at the store. My adrenaline paused for a split second. *Our store is on fire.*

One look at Ruth's eyes and I started weeping. She squared her face to mine and grabbed my shoulders. "Lindsay! Stop crying! Stop it! Wipe your face off and get over there and tell them what to do."

It's what had to be done and what I needed to hear. I bolted right back across the street and talked with a police officer. Red trucks began peeling into the street and surrounding the store. Volunteer firefighters were blocking roads, and racing to the firehouse a few blocks up to grab gear and return to swap spots. I did a run-down of anything I thought might explode under heat; the feed would just burn, the propane tanks? That was about it.

Now, having done everything I could, I was officially in the way. Pam and I sat across the street comforted by the company of a few locals; a coat for Pam, and water. I don't remember how long it was before I called my mom and she arrived, but the snow began to fall.

My mind finally began to slow down to the speed of my body. I was staring at firemen as they cut holes in our garage doors and pried open the brand new steel door to our soon-to-be kitchen. The community of friends and onlookers had grown. Cell phones aimed, clicked and recorded. Vulnerable, but I wasn't angry or defeated or scared. I felt a weird peace, and strangely calm, almost out-of-body. Fire trucks kept arriving. The snow grew heavier and otherwise, pretty.

Nathan's big red truck flew into the gas station across the street. I always admire how cool, calm and collected he looks in the middle of crazy. I met him half way. We leaned into each other and watched as they worked. No words. We'd reached about an inch of snow on the ground, so I decided to go sit in the van in the heat.

God is good. God is bigger. That's all I kept thinking. I looked at my phone where there were several texts and messages. *Don't look yet.* I needed to post something to tell people we were okay. Instagram stories. Basically I posted, "We are safe. God is good and He is in control."

Tell the girls. I need to be the one to tell the girls.

I buzzed into the school office and was greeted with a hug and half pitiful, half compassionate eyes.

When the girls stepped out of their classroom, I met their confused eyes from around the corner of the foyer. With my mom next to me, we gathered them around a bench in the office.

"I wanted to be the first to tell you guys that we had a fire at the feed store today. No one was hurt and the firefighters are bravely taking care of it, but many people may start talking about it, and I want you to know, directly from me, that it's going to be just fine. We don't need to worry about it."

Tessa interrupted, eyes wide, "What about the scooter?"

"And the bike!" Ruthie piped in.

I grinned. The girls were going to be just fine. They showed no fear of the unknown or for their security. I needed their simple, adolescent perspective and the affirmation that I too had nothing to fear. My heart calmed. *Thank you God for prompting me to be the one to tell them.*

Mom explained how they were all going to hop in her van, swing by and get Joanna at daycare, then head to her house "until Mom and Dad are done working with the firefighters."

Heading back to the store seemed so normal, but when I arrived, smelled the smoke and allowed myself to anticipate damage, my stomach re-fell. I reached out to pick up my phone ... *No, I'm not ready to look.*

Back in the gas station parking lot, directly across the street from the store, I fished a stocking cap from the back seat of Nathan's truck, and stood with him, Nick's wife, Jackie, and my brothers (in-law). We anxiously waited to get inside the building and assess our loss. Back when Nathan and I first bought the store, his parents bought the entire city block, which about fifteen years prior, had been a car dealership. Nathan and I were using the former showroom as a feed store. The warehouse, formerly the service area, was used by the Wineinger family and back stock for feed. At the end of the building, we'd built a wall and Nick ran a tire shop in the last service bay area. Chad stored equipment for his landscaping business in what used to be the detailing garage. Nick's tire store had definitely acquired some damage from the forceful hose water and Chad, hopefully, would "only" have some smoke damage.

During a remodel, what looked like three separate buildings had been joined under one roof with some gaps here and there and in between; gaps, which we later found out, had saved our store from being burned totally to the ground.

At about 5:30 that evening, I drove to Mom and Dad's to check in. The girls were running around in dress-up dresses. Remnant pizza smells wafted over empty boxes. I reminded Ruthie she had some reading to do while I flipped on the news. A news station hatchback had been at the fire, so I watched just in case. Sure enough, the TV flashed pictures of our burning store as they reported a very ill-informed story. I wished they would have approached one of us to get accurate information.

My blood wanted to boil, but I rolled my eyes, calmed myself and let Mom know I was headed back out. I threw on my extra layers, preparing for the cold and snow; more snow now, and I caught a whiff of smoke from my jacket. That smell.

Back at Casey's, our local gas station, convenience store and pizzeria owner brought out a pile of steaming boxes. Pizza for the firefighters, still working, and for those of us watching and waiting.

We got our first chance to walk inside. Other than a haze, most things seemed untouched. With sirens off and the shouting and running over, I heard an eerie quiet. A pink, goo-like substance dripped down the big, loading door. Melted insulation still poured through the seams. Pam's wet paint bubbled on the wall.

By now, we could see that the worst part was on the wall between the warehouse and the feed store. Besides that, no visible damage inside. I think that's when the silence broke and we could talk.

A few days later, we would learn that all the feed in the store and warehouse was ruined. Because we were unsure how high the temperatures were raised and what chemicals were released from the different variety of materials in the warehouse, liability required us to throw away every item of feed and food. Three chest freezers full of beef, chicken and pork (we just filled the day before) were now considered unsellable. Tarnished. Anything the smoke touched…wasted.

But at that given moment, the only question I had was, "What now?"

By 6:30 p.m., the different fire stations were calling their trucks home. Everything was under control. Hoses were being rolled up. One truck and hose stuck around. As they found hot spots, they would hose them down, and a worker from the township used a skid steer to haul and drop bucket after bucket of soaked pine shavings and hay.

Maybe it was my stomach talking to me, but watching that worker reminded me of how a chef drops a glob of something on a plate and uses the back of a serving spoon to smoosh it out. A chef might know a more technical term, but I wondered if that term might apply to pine shavings and the back of a skid bucket.

Looking around, I was in awe; not the good kind. I saw the remaining wood frames of thirty booths we had just purchased and stored on pallet racking. I had just finished up the layout of the restaurant dining room the day before and was working on wall decor. The windows in Nick's newly remodeled office were blown out from the water pressure of the fire hose. After seeing all this, I still can't complain about a thing; I'm thankful.

I drew a line with my finger in the residue of the glass that covered our pie refrigerator case. Jake had just finished repairing it. The taillights on the box truck were droopy from melting under the heat of the flames. I empathized with that heartless piece of equipment. We traipsed through about four inches of water as we assessed the impact and then we looked up. The massive steel beams supporting the roof curved slightly to the south.

The fire was just that hot.

I was no longer of use there. I met Nathan's eyes and told him I was leaving. The girls needed to be home soon anyway. They had school in the morning. The snow was accumulating again and making me nervous.

Like many times before, I got to Mom and Dad's and rallied up the girls, and we left. It was dark by then, but I needed the girls to say goodnight to Nathan, or maybe I wasn't quite ready to let go, so I prepared them for the drive-by. "The store is going to look different."

Darkness shielded the majority of destruction, but they saw the burned contents from the warehouse on the front drive. Nathan came out long enough to give each of them kisses, and we made our way out of town toward home.

When I turned into our driveway, it was as if we hit auto pilot. We made our way into the kitchen. "Don't dump your book bags on the floor!" I barked. Ruthie and Tessa fed Moose, our lab. They scurried to the bathroom to brush their teeth and change into PJs. They grabbed a snack and hit the couch for some TV before bed.

I sat at the edge of my bed. *Breathe. I'm home. We're all safe.* How bizarre. I felt mentally prepared to turn on my phone. Lots of texts, lots of messages, loads of people praying. *God, speak please. Not me.* And so I did another InstaStory.

Nathan made it home. We put the girls to bed. Then, Nathan and I took turns. He responded to messages while I showered, and then switch. We started a list of who needed to call whom in the morning.

By 9:30 p.m., (that's early for us) we were lying in bed. He grabbed my hand and held on. No words. I silently streaked my cheeks with tears, not out of emotion, but from sheer overwhelm. I'd started this day in this very position, petitioning to God; and I found myself laying there yet again, stunned and speechless by His handy work. A chaotic day bookended by normalcy, but in my heart, a love for the everyday stuff, tenfold.

–Lindsay Wineinger

More than Two of Us

I knew more about God and church than most people do when they choose to follow Jesus. I should have. I went to a Christian college, was a leader in our church's youth group, and taught a Sunday school class. Plus, I was a pastor's wife.

When I was thirty-two and our congregation was challenged to pray through a list of sins, I did. I named those sins silently and considered the ones I had done. Then God spoke to me, almost audibly. He told me I needed to surrender my life to Him. So, I did. My life changed from knowing a lot about God to having a personal relationship with Him.

People make assumptions when they learn I'm a pastor's wife. They suddenly have expectations. But I've learned to assume nothing and gage my expectations by what God says in His Word, what my husband and family need, and how I can best serve through our local church. Or that is my ideal.

When I tell people my husband pastors a small church, most of them have no idea what that means. When I say "small," people tend to picture *Little House on the Prairie* small—seventy-five to one-hundred people clustered in family groups and singing traditional hymns.

How small is our church? The church we currently serve averages six or seven on Sunday mornings. That's not six or seven families, but six or seven people. Their average age is seventy-five, making me the youngest active member at the age of sixty. If one of us is sick or gone for any reason, we won't have a quorum and need to reschedule our business meetings. When it's time to elect officers, committees and teachers of the church, we don't struggle to form a nominating committee. We are the committee! Three of our active members have died during the eleven years my husband, Victor, has been pastor. They are truly missed for their service and sorely missed as friends.

Some question why we keep the doors open, and I must admit to asking that same thing on occasion. But God always nudges my heart and I see clearly the purpose He has, not only for Victor, but for me. If God knows the number of hairs on my head, surely He sees the little deeds we do for a small group of His faithful saints. It's about more than Victor and me.

When you serve God in a country church the size of ours, and even some larger churches, the congregation often can't afford to hire a full-time pastor, so the pastor works a regular job to support himself and his family. Mondays through Fridays, Victor is program manager for a social services agency and works to help young people get into school and find jobs. Nights and weekends are for taking care of his family.

Church members often become an extension of the pastor's family. If the church door is open, he is leading, teaching or preaching. And when it is closed, he's got study and preparation to do. That's a lot to do between mowing the lawn and taking out the trash. Victor is what they call a bivocational pastor.

Until recently, I was the site director for Head Start at their Southern Illinois University campus. After twenty-two years, I am semi-retired and working part-time at a Christian day care as an office assistant. Victor and I both landed in careers that serve young people; yet even while I was a teenager, God made a special place in my heart for senior adults that needed to be satisfied. You've probably heard it said that God has a sense of humor. Well, I'm telling you He invented the concept of irony, too. He makes all things right—eventually.

Our church isn't packed on Sunday mornings or Wednesday nights, but the place in my heart created for older folks is always full. To say I don't miss a bigger church would be a lie. In fact, Victor and I coordinate a ministry to churches for the Illinois Baptist State Association (IBSA) called Lay Renewal. Its purpose is to inspire and equip church members for maximizing the growth of God's Kingdom. The evidence that we've been successful in this ministry goes deeper than numbers, but the irony that God can use the two of us to help grow churches? I'm astounded.

After one of those weekends with louder music and kids running around, we're ready for a little love from our little (and older) congregation. Almost every Sunday I take home a treat. It might be a bag of candy for my grandkids, a kitchen towel, or something anyone who loves an avid St Louis Cardinals fan (Victor) can't leave Goodwill without! We know what it means to be content in our small, country church.

Our contentment didn't happen overnight. We've been married forty years, and Victor has been a minister for most of those years. He started as a youth pastor. The first church where he was the "senior" pastor had about twenty-five members of various ages. We were a young family of six, four of us under the age of five. Until we walked in, the youngest attender was a seven-year-old. The church ladies got together. They painted, decorated and bought a crib and toys for a nursery. My six-month-old and two-year-old were very much loved.

We lived about thirty minutes from the church and had to be there Sunday mornings, Sunday evenings, and Wednesday evenings. It wasn't easy getting all of us ready and to church on time! Several of the senior adults would prepare a lunch after church and invite us to stay the afternoon so we didn't have to put so many miles on our car or cut short our naptime. My love for seniors grew.

I wasn't always so confident and outgoing.

One Wednesday evening I was downstairs with the kids while Victor was upstairs leading a prayer meeting. The phone rang, so I answered it. The message was for Victor and couldn't wait until he had dismissed the group. I had to go upstairs to deliver the news. Only a handful of members were present, and I knew them all, but I was scared to death. Silly I know, but I trembled during the walk upstairs, while I interrupted the meeting, and until I was safe downstairs with the children.

And I made mistakes.

We had about seven or eight children in Sunday school one morning. This was at the second church where Victor was pastor. Again, this was a small church and all the children (aged four to ten) were in the same class. As the teacher, I was tasked with telling the story, using a game or activity to review the Bible story, guiding my students in some sort of craft, and maintaining control while I encouraged the memorization of the week's Bible verse.

The older girls didn't want to listen or cooperate. After several warnings they kept interrupting and distracting the younger ones. I threatened to have them go sit with their parents if they kept misbehaving. Well, I finally had to follow through and sent them to their parents. Some parents got very upset with me and things were never right again.

Funny things happen, too. But I can't always tell. It's not that I've taken a vow of silence or signed an oath of confidentiality. God holds me to a standard. My life and story is never far from family—my church family.

I haven't met a pastor's wife who hasn't, at one time or another, wanted to slip into a church, worship God with a song and a prayer, then hear The Word preached and go home without concern that a church member might feel offended or slighted. Not to brag, but it takes a special kind of lady to see what I see and do what I do as the wife of a bivocational pastor.

It takes a mature congregation who loves Jesus more than anything to see what they see and do what they do for a bivocational pastor like Victor and a pastor's wife, like me.

–Holly Templeton Duckworth

Drive and Determination

I was a stay-at-home mom, partly by choice, and partly because I was afraid of change. I had been trying to decide whether to play it safe and leave my life the way it was or try something I'd been thinking about for a long time.

My challenge was waiting in the driveway: our brand new, blue Ford Escort. Could I meet that challenge? I hoped. It had been eighteen years since I had driven a standard (stick shift) car. Even then, I only drove one once or twice with a friend's father, but I had often regretted not knowing how.

Before I tackled driving in busy city traffic with three young passengers, I wanted to take the car out into the country and practice with no one witnessing my every move.

My husband was working late on this particular afternoon, leaving it up to me to get our eleven-year-old daughter, Debbie, to the orthodontist whose office is in a large, neighboring city. Her braces were hurting her mouth so I couldn't put my fate off to another day. Her appointment was at the busiest time of the afternoon, and there were several hills between our house and the orthodontist. The ten miles of country didn't scare me as much as the last five miles of city traffic.

I had no choice. Asking my mother to take us was out of the question. She was against us buying a stick shift car in the first place, and I didn't want to admit a fear of driving my own car. I had spent an entire afternoon defending the purchase of that shiny Ford.

"A stick shift car gets better gas mileage and has fewer things to go wrong on it than an automatic!"

My pride wouldn't let me ask her for help. I would manage somehow.

Nine-year-old Nicole and six-year-old Michael scooted into the back seat, buckled up, and waited for the action to start. Their little faces looked back at me through the rearview mirror. Debbie, as the oldest, sat next to me with apprehension all over her preteen face.

"Mom, are you sure you can drive this?" she asked. Her confidence in me was less than overwhelming.

"Of course," I lied.

I killed the engine twice before I got out of the driveway.

"That's not too bad," I said to myself. "Relax! You can do it."

Unbelievably, I shifted all the way into fourth without grinding any gears. My tension eased a little.

Cole Hollow Road was a curvy, two-lane blacktop where country homes and cornfields provide a great atmosphere for a mind to wander. But I was concentrating on getting my daughter to the orthodontist without a major accident.

"I'd better start slowing down and turn on my left turn signal. Let's see, put on the brake and the clutch. Now shift down to third. Wonderful. No oncoming cars. I can turn without coming to a complete stop. That ninety degree curve is ahead. I better shift all the way down to second. I'm getting the hang of this!"

As usual, my children ignored me. Nicole and Michael fussed with each other and Debbie sang along with the radio. It's a normal day, a beautiful fall day, and there are no stop signs for at least a mile or two.

The three way stop at the edge of the city was a breeze; I didn't even jerk the car when I took off. So proud of myself in that moment, I forgot about the next stop sign, just ahead, and on a steep incline. Traffic on route 150, a major artery into the city, sped across my line of vision as I approached.

"How am I ever going to make a left hand turn across that busy highway? Maybe traffic will thin down before I get to the stop sign." With no place to turn around and no other way, I was committed.

I stopped at the sign and told the children, "Keep your heads back and keep quiet."

My husband had told me that when I had to stop on an incline, to use the clutch and the gas pedal to keep the car stopped, "Not the brake." But I was nervous and forgot. Too late. My right foot was holding that brake pedal to the floor.

"Oh no." I said to myself. "Now the car will roll backwards when I take off, but as long as no one comes up behind me, I'll be all right."

I watched for my chance. "There it is. Take my right foot off the brake and punch the gas pedal. Quick. Before the car rolls backwards."

The engine died. "Now what?" I hit the brake, held my breath, then turned the key and restarted the engine. I waited for my second chance to jump onto route 150. Again, the car stalled.

Using her frightened voice, Debbie yelled, "Mom, there's a police car behind us."

Nicole repeated (in case I hadn't heard), "There's a police car behind us, what are we going to do?"

I looked at the rearview mirror and there he was, staring at me from no more than three feet behind my rear bumper. Other cars began pulling up behind the police car.

"Mom, what are you going to do?" "Are we going to get arrested?" "How embarrassing!" My passengers cluttered the car and my mind with their voices.

"Hush! All of you."

I remembered my husband also saying, "Put on the hand brake if the car stalls on an incline. Your right foot will be free to regulate the gas pedal. Then, once the motor is regulated, take off the hand brake and go."

"All right. The hand brake is on and the car is running smoothly."

During all this, I managed to remember the next busy intersection. It had an equally challenging ramp. The tension inside me climbed, but so did my determination.

"Make a right turn, Judy!" I said to myself. "There's more than one way to get to that dental office."

A gap in traffic gave me opportunity to turn right, but now, I couldn't get the emergency brake to release. The police officer was still behind me, and watching.

"Please don't get out of your car. I've got this!"

Our brand-new Ford jerked and squealed, leaving a dark trail of rubber on the street. I hear a "finally" come from the back seat.

I hoped he wouldn't come after me for squealing my tires, but thought he was probably too busy laughing. Embarrassed and frustrated, my tears came unchecked.

Barely through the intersection, traffic stopped suddenly and I slammed on the brakes. Killed the engine again. After two tries and an "Oh no, not again," from Debbie, I got the car started and we were moving forward.

At this point, I'm shaking so badly that I can hardly drive at all. Between the battle going on in my head, and the tears, I could only see this day ending badly.

I screeched, "Shut up, all I want to do is go home."

If I turn back now, will I ever get over the embarrassment or shame of giving up? But if I go on, can I make it?

My decision made, I screamed, "All right! I want everyone to keep their mouth closed until we reach the orthodontist's office."

I felt more strength of determination seeping through, gradually replacing my nervous tension. I managed to merge, without an incident, up a hill into multiple lanes of traffic. Two more obstacles were between me and the orthodontist. Another merge, up a ramp, onto yet another busy street and the stop light on the hill in front of the doctor's office. If I have to stop at either of these places … well, I knew what would probably happen.

With the tension in me starting to subside, I could now talk calmly to the children and ease some of their fear. A generous space opened up and I merged uphill, like any other big-city driver. Nicole and Michael were starting to play now, but Debbie stayed frozen in her seat, watching every move I made and every move of the traffic around us.

The red light in front of the orthodontist's office miraculously changed to green as I slowed down and prepared for a stop. Cars ahead of me began to move. Thankfully, another opening at the entrance to the parking lot; I turned without stopping. As I parked the car, I realized how tightly I had been gripping the steering wheel and said a silent prayer of gratefulness.

I looked at my watch, wondering how late all the stopping and stalling and my last minute detour had made us, then laughed. We were five minutes early.

A warm glow came over me, something like what a long-distance runner must feel as he crosses the finish line. *I did it!*

Debbie got her braces adjusted and was no longer in pain. Nicole and Michael had a story to tell, although I hoped they wouldn't tell it. And, our trip home was uneventful. The three of us, and that shiny, blue Escort, had survived.

It wasn't long after that trip to the orthodontist that I conquered another fear. Sixteen years after my high school graduation, I started back to school. More importantly, I had conquered the desire to always give up when the going gets rough.

I'm thankful for what this experience taught me. I no longer had to sit in my house hiding behind a mask of motherhood. I've seen first-hand how God can use a little drive and determination.

–Judy Mandrell

When What You Want to Say Won't. Come. Out.

… At least not in the *way* you want.

I read blogs and think, "I could do that!"

Back when there were actual magazines, I'd subscribed to many of them, and always thought it looked so easy. *I talk the same way they do. I could make my point and be funny, articulate, and interesting.* Easy!

Not so much.

Here I sit with a perfectly good Word document right in front of me, blank and just waiting to be filled with all manner of wisdom, encouragement, or thoughts provoking people to think and grow.

Annnnd crickets.

Part of my problem (and I own this) is continuity. I'll have a great thought in my head, then a paragraph or two in, and I'm down a rabbit hole only to surface with a totally different thought.

Connection is key, context is your friend. I tell myself these things …

I'm not formally educated outside of a high school diploma, but have always been a voracious reader (Thanks, Dad!), so an additional issue is probably grammar, or at the very least, punctuation.

I love commas and ellipses, in case you couldn't tell …

Another problem is the writing itself. These days, writers use a combination of proper English language and text-speak. I'm old enough not to fall into the latter too much. I still can't wrap my mind around the fact that by adding just two more letters "u" could have an entire word. Why don't "you" use them? "B4" I go too far. Get the picture?

I know just enough of the mechanics of the English language to be dangerous. I type the way I talk, and if there's a pause in my sentence, hello comma. Probably not the "correct" way to punctuate …

I'm in my (very) early sixties, and one would think I'd have *something* to say. My good Lord knows I've made my share (okay, more than my fair share) of mistakes. There should be at least something along those lines to write about, right? I've also been a born-again follower of Jesus Christ for about fifty of those sixty-plus years. Surely, somewhere along the way God has given me some wisdom to share, right? Triumph over hard-fought battles. Lessons learned! Faith increased! God glorified in the midst of wrong turns taken.

Why won't these things *come out*?

I'm pretty good at inserting my foot in my mouth, and adept at ungodly responses. Thoughtless comments can spew from me at the speed of light. Why can't anything *constructive* make its way out?

I spoke with my friend who is a published author. She seems to think I'm a writer. She says, "Just write like you speak. Tell about how you deal with an ordinary day. Please don't stretch to reach for the profound or exciting."

She went on to tell me about an exercise that an editor assigned during a class she attended. The editor had them write a short story, using nothing but one-syllable words. As my friend noticed the blank look on my face, she explained. "It's weird," she said. "When you take big words and profound concepts out of the equation, the story has room to shine."

Well, I do want to write, so I figured I'd try it. My husband is fertile ground for stories (should've thought of that sooner). See! My friend's advice is already helping.

'Shrooms (Morrell, not Magic): An Exercise in One-Syllable Writing

My husband, T. J., waits all year for the first signs of spring. Not for the rose or the lark, green grass or rain, but for those 'shrooms which are so scarce and hard to find.

He looks high and low, far and wide, yet they hide from him well. One friend will find eight or nine, and some friends will find more. "Why not me?" he might think. "This can't be!"

Be it rain or shine, heat or cold, he will search the ground, year by year with no luck at all. What can he do? He *must* have those 'shrooms—to cook and eat as well as share! "Bring some to church," is a thought he has shared.

So T. J. thinks … tap-tap-tap … there must be a way.

A bulb lights up! A thought is born! With a smile and a nod, T. J. knows just what to do. He's a man with a plan. "This year, I'll win the game and out-fox those 'shrooms! I'll make my own," he says to the air (when I'm not at home—and at times when I am!).

He went down stairs to the room "just for him" where he sets up his "lab." He mixed a bit of this and added a bit of that. Then he waits …

In just two short days he had his wish, 'shroom juice to spread 'neath a tree where small crowns will soon pop up from the earth on their way to be a rare prize of great worth (to him).

'Shrooms!!

He says God gave him a brain—and yes, faith, but it's good to show God how we can think, use what God gives to form a plan and then take it to its end.

Facebook (proper noun = freebie on the one-syllable rule) is next. He posted his grand plan, though not for show or gain. It's in his blood to teach and share; that's what T. J. does.

I pray there's no big mess (as with most of his "grand plans"), but I know how this makes him feel; the joy it brings, so I try not to see what should soon be out of the house.

I guess it's sad that I don't like 'shrooms. T. J. would love for me to love them. But hey, that just means more for him!

The end.

Well, that wasn't as hard as I'd thought it would be. I emailed my story and my friend said she liked it. While I had my doubts, I do know she taught me a valuable lesson. And she was right, I don't need to worry about being profound or exciting.

I've often heard it said, "Write what you know." The short story exercise about T. J. showed me the truth in that. Even though it was a small exercise and the words fairly flowed … Okay, except for racking my brain for one-syllable alternatives, the concept flowed.

I haven't prayed about this as much as I've thought about it, and that's actually very telling. I know better than to do *anything* without prayer.

Colossians 4:2 (ESV) tells us to "Continue steadfastly in prayer."

I know better than to do otherwise!

So, going forward and "praying without ceasing" (1 Thessalonians 5:17, ESV) I'll see what God leads me to say.

If *He* can't get it out of me, no one can …

–Susan Walker

Teach Me, Lord, to Wait

I stared at the computer screen. Nearly two dozen open tabs at the top of my browser were all about "starting the adoption process." Fifteen minutes into this whole adoption thing, and I already felt overwhelmed. My husband, David, had his laptop open doing the same Google searches.

"Where do we even start?" he asked.

"I have no idea."

At the time, I just wanted a map of God's plan, but as all adoptive parents know, the pathway to adoption is full of detours, delays, and a lot of faith in God's perfect timing. If such a map actually existed and I had known every little detail that would need to fall into place perfectly, I probably would have deemed it impossible and given up. Thankfully, God led us step by baby step and minute by minute.

I was diagnosed with PCOS (polycystic ovary syndrome) in my twenties and my body never quite figured out the whole reproductive cycle, so I knew having biological children would be difficult for me. We tried fertility treatments for a short time, but I hated the mood swings, constant monitoring, and biweekly blood draws, so after a few "failed" months, we decided to pursue adoption. Early in our dating relationship, we had talked about adopting a child, and we knew God was calling us to adopt. This was an easy decision for us, but we thought we would have biological children first.

A few months after this decision, God led David to pastor a small church in rural southern Illinois, which meant moving to another state. He had a family friend in Illinois who was a social worker for the Baptist Children's

Home—one of God's little graces throughout the process. We put the Google searches behind us and contacted her to start the process.

The first step was to fill out the home-study paperwork. My goal was to complete it within three months, but moving to a new state, starting a new job, and getting to know a new church made the paperwork take closer to seven months. In the grand scheme of things, seven months isn't a long time, but when your heart is set on holding a new baby, it feels endless.

In the meantime, I was faced with coming to terms with my infertility. It seemed like Facebook was filled with birth announcements, TV was filled with baby ads, and friends were all having kids the old-fashioned way. I spent many nights feeling sorry for myself—crying and questioning God's plan. All I wanted was to be a mom, but that dream seemed unattainable. Why did I have to provide my last three years of tax returns, go through over forty hours of training, have a health physical, background check, and provide a letter from my employer to have a baby while that random lady in line behind me at the grocery store had four kids she couldn't even keep track of? I was angry. In my heart, I knew God was good, but in my mind, I thought he was withholding good.

Meanwhile, David was experiencing his own adoption journey.

Like many infertile Christian women, I related to Hannah in the Bible. I read her story in the beginning of First Samuel over and over. I felt her humiliation as her husband's second wife provoked her for not having a child. I knew her anguish as she begged God for a son. I understood the tension between wanting a child and being content with the love of her husband. One day as I was reading, I got caught up in Hannah's prayer. She said, "If you give me a son, then I will give him to you all the days of his life."

I could hear my own prayers when I read Hannah's. *If you do this …*

God didn't need Hannah to dedicate Samuel to his service. Maybe it wasn't about the child, but about Hannah's willingness to give up the child. Hannah was so desperate for a son, she was willing to give him to God's work. Desperation led her to loosen her grip and give it to God.

I felt awful for trying to be a victim of my infertility and focusing on "what could have been." God listened through my disappointment and anger until I slowly stopped comparing my story to everyone else's and started seeing what an amazing gift He was giving us through adoption. After all, the moment I became a Christian, God adopted me. I am so blessed to get a miniscule and earthly glimpse into that type of love.

It took almost a year to get through the entire home study process which included physicals, multiple interviews, ten letters of reference, and more background checks than I even knew existed. With the help of the social worker at the Baptist Children's Home, we chose to pursue a private, domestic adoption. At the beginning of May we were officially "home study approved," so we chose to send our information to a few private adoption lawyers and set up our adoption website. We also put the word out to friends and acquaintances that we were wanting to adopt in case they knew of an expectant mother who was considering adoption. Finally, we were officially in the "sit-and-wait" phase.

The social worker told us, and the literature repeated, "Some families stay in this stage for a few weeks and others for a few years. There really is no way to know how long it will be before you are chosen as an adoptive family."

In the beginning, we were optimistic and patient. We kept an eye open for potential adoptions, reached out to a few expectant mothers, and trusted that God would take care of things. Every ten to fourteen days we would get updates and learn we had not been chosen. Rejection was expected, but never easy. At the beginning of August, I returned to teaching. I reminded my principal that we were adopting, emphasizing the chance I would need to take a leave of absence at some unknown point during the school year.

One week into the school year, in the middle of fourth class period, my phone rang. I normally have my phone on silent, but apparently had forgotten that day. I went to check it and saw that it was our adoption case worker. My high school students were finishing a pre-test, and I had an aide in the classroom, so I stepped into the closet to take the call. An expectant mom had looked at our profile and wanted us to adopt her baby! This was really happening.

The next night, we talked on the phone with Noel (not her real name). She was expecting a baby girl in mid-September. Five weeks away. David and I talked with her for about an hour and it all clicked into place. She was incredibly kind and easy to talk to. We learned a little about her upbringing and her hopes for her baby.

It was a Thursday when we signed papers and faxed them to Noel's lawyer. Adoption training had prepared us for the large sum of money needed, and we were within a few thousand dollars. At this point, since the birth was coming up so quickly, we learned that we would owe a large sum of money in only a few days. God had already provided the greatest portion of the money. Eight years earlier, before I had even met David, I bought and renovated a house. When we moved to Illinois, we sold the house, and the equity provided most of what we needed. We were still a few thousand dollars short of the necessary amount. All week long we looked into loans and grants. David and I called our parents and grandparents who were more than willing to help, but the logistics of getting the money from one account to another in time was overwhelming. We prayed about it, but we had no clue how we were going to wire the full amount by the deadline.

The morning the money was due, I woke up to get ready for school, and decided to check our bank account again. The excess money from my student loan for my doctoral program had been deposited overnight. It was $117.00 more than we needed, and a total surprise. Normally, I accepted only the amount I needed for school expenses and returned the excess. However, in the chaos of starting the school year, I had forgotten to fill out the form a month earlier, before we even knew about this baby. God had a plan.

We spent the weekend buying baby stuff, and on Monday there was a historical solar eclipse. My school chose to close for the day, so I was home with David. We went outside and witnessed the eclipse with our neighbors. As the sun was reappearing, Noel called. She was at her doctor's office, experiencing complications. A sonogram at that visit showed that she was actually expecting a boy. Our weekend shopping trip, as fun as it was, left us with pink polka dot sheets and piles of ruffles and floral. Thankfully, we had picked out a navy crib, so that was good to go.

Noel begged, “Please don't be mad at me. I didn't know!”

It took me a second to realize she was apologizing for telling us the wrong gender. "We're happy with whatever God gives us.”

She sighed a breath of relief and said, “I was afraid you would change your mind.”

"No chance of that happening!”

She went on to tell us that her doctors were monitoring her closely because she was losing fluid. "There's a chance I'll have an emergency C-section this evening.”

We packed our bags, but our case worker assured us, "This happens all the time. It will be a few more weeks."

Noel called later that night to say that she was doing better, and she had a follow-up appointment Thursday morning. At that appointment they would schedule her C-section.

We were anxious about the health of Noel and her baby, but ultimately, God gave us both a lot of peace. Thursday morning, Noel called me in the middle of my first class period. I was expecting her call, and had told my students I would need to take it. They were rushing her into surgery because her fluids kept dropping. A fourteen-hour drive separated us.

Our bags were packed, so David was able to grab them, pick me up at school, and we were on our way. The day before, my long-term sub had shadowed me all day, so she knew what to expect. I had just signed paperwork for my maternity leave. No worry about my students or my job while I was away. God's timing? He *did (perfectly) in nine days what would have taken me nine months.*

About three hours later, while we were driving, the call came that our son had been born. Arriving at the hospital later that night, and walking into the maternity unit, all I could think was, "Don't faint." We were given security badges and greeted by Noel's family. Baby Boy (as his birth certificate said) was handed to us.

He was a tiny baby, with a handsome, squished up face and a head full of hair. I wish I had words to describe meeting him for the first time, but all I can say is our smiles were huge and our hearts were full. The nerves were gone. The rushed drive was over. I was witnessing a miracle.

When I went through infertility treatments, a doctor had said, "The odds of you becoming a mom are nearly impossible," and while she clearly meant the odds of me having a biological child, it still resonated with me throughout this process. Thankfully I serve a God who does the impossible. We named our son Andrew, after the disciple, because the few times Andrew is mentioned in the Bible, he is bringing people to meet Jesus.

Our little man needed to spend some time in the NICU and Noel was still recovering from delivery, so we were able to spend precious time getting to know our baby's birth mom. The day she was discharged she signed papers and made statements that gave us the biggest gift a person can give—her baby boy. We sat in the hallway waiting for her lawyer to meet with us, and

I kept thinking about John 3:16 (KJV), "For God so loved the world that He gave His only begotten Son." While I can't imagine what it's like for Noel, I am grateful for her gift of love and sacrifice.

We were hoping it would be a five-day NICU stay for Andrew, but a few days in we learned we would be there for about three weeks. We made hotel arrangements and settled into our role as parents of a NICU baby. We spent every waking moment at the hospital and many sleepless nights. Between our time with Andrew, rushing out for food and giving our parents updates, we caught glimpses of news, here and there.

At the ten-day mark, a hurricane threatened the state. Store shelves were empty and gas supplies were dwindling. We began preparing to "hunker down" by searching for water and keeping our gas tank full. Both of us had grown up in the Midwest, so we had no clue how to prepare for a hurricane.

By God's grace, Andrew improved faster than anticipated. We learned he would get discharged after only thirteen days in the NICU, and three days before the hurricane was expected to hit. My mom flew in the day before he was to be discharged, so she was there to help us his first night out of the hospital. The process of getting court approval for interstate travel with a newly adopted child typically takes six to ten days, but one day later, we got word that we could leave the state due to the impending weather emergency.

Now, we were torn between staying and possibly experiencing a hurricane or driving home and leaving Mom behind. Her return flight to Missouri wasn't scheduled for another few days and our small car was packed. We had all been looking for flights home for her, but the hurricane had everything booked. Ultimately, we decided to drive back to Illinois and avoid the storm.

The night we left, mom decided to go to the airport. One seat was available on a non-stop flight to Missouri that night.

Just like Hannah, crying out in the temple begging God for a son, adopting Andrew had me waiting down on my knees multiple times. When I look back at the process as a whole, I can see God's intricacy in every detail. He loves me enough to weave together a story that not only ended with the best gift of being a mom, but also gently pushed me to grow in faith. Andrew is a constant reminder of God's goodness and His amazing gift of love.

–Jenny Auxier

The New Teacher

My hometown elementary school hired me to be a floating third grade teacher. No, I wouldn't be a levitating apparition, I would be moving from classroom to classroom helping the other ten third grade teachers by pulling small groups from their oversized classes to do reading and math instruction.

I thought, "Why not just give me my own classroom and alleviate that overcrowding?" Then I was told, "There's simply no more space in the building."

So, I was ecstatic to have landed my first public school position and felt up to the challenge of supporting these teachers, some of whom had known me as a kid.

The week of welcome-back activities prepped my mind for the work ahead since I had no space of my own to plan. When I arrived at school on the Friday before school started, the principal called me into her office.

"Good news!" she said. "The schoolboard has decided to add you as a full classroom teacher! We're going to create a temporary classroom for you in The Nest! We're building a classroom for you that will be ready by November."

I couldn't even say words, so I blindly followed her down the hall and out the door to my new room. Don't let it fool you because it surely sounds homey, but, "The Nest" was the name given to the old high school AG building—AG as in agriculture. The aging pole barn was probably 400 yards from the elementary school building's back doors. It was currently home to the entire sixth grade, considered middle school in my school district. We made the hike across the grass and entered the building and my classroom. I was instantly dismayed.

The room was quite big and had something like a bar (yes, the kind with alcoholic drinks) in the back corner. The desks had probably been there when I attended this school and were covered in grime. They ranged in size from kindergartener to high school football player. A window along the back wall of the room looked into the garage where, at one time, AG students learned about farm equipment. Now it was used as storage. This looked nothing like a warm inviting place to grow young minds. My principal patted me on the back and told me how exciting this was. With a warm smile and her ever professional air, she left me in the room, alone. I took a deep breath.

Where to begin?

Okay. My teacher desk was in a very poor location, so I started pushing it across the room to a new spot. I put both hands on the desk, put my back into it and gave it a good shove. Two legs broke off the desk. At that moment I was overwhelmed with the impossibility of my task and began to sob. I'm not sure how long I sat there crying on the floor. I cried tears of disappointment grieving the loss of all the plans I had made already for the previously assigned duties. I cried tears of inundation because I had no idea how on earth to even start sorting through my emotions, much less begin the process of planning for a classroom full of children in three short days. I cried tears of inadequacy because I didn't think I was up for this challenge. I'm not sure what I spent the day doing besides attempting to put my desk back together through teary eyes.

My third grade teammates did their best to get me ready for the first week's curriculum. I had just a few hours to find out what I needed to know to teach the kids what they needed to know as well as make copies and nab as many supplies and classroom items as I could scrounge from the leftovers of any teacher who would donate to me. I tried my best to listen and absorb what they were saying, but I was in an absolute daze.

I can't remember exactly what prompted me to do it. It was very likely the level-headed thinking of one of my sisters. I highly doubt I was able to put together enough unoccupied brain cells to think of such a brilliant plan. I called a friend from college who had been teaching third grade for three years already. I hadn't seen her in those three years because after college I spent some time teaching at a private school in Moscow, Russia and doing some missionary work. So, I wasn't sure what my friend could do to help me, other than walk through the steps to get me started on a path.

The next morning she and her amazing mom, two beautiful Christian women, drove an hour from home and showed up at my classroom door armed with glue guns, poster board, lesson plans, overhead transparencies, and everything that would make my classroom what it needed to be. They worked with me—all day—getting things on the walls, covering that terrible window, finding a way to make the bar look like a purposeful storage area, and generally helping me pull things together. While we worked, she taught me strategies that I'm still using, twenty-three years later, to build community among the students in my classroom. By the end of my day, Linny and her mom had me saying, "This is possible."

My sisters came to help me finish the job on Sunday, and on Monday morning when the students walked into my classroom it was a comfortable home. We stayed in that room until November, then as promised, we moved into a newly renovated classroom that had been garage storage under the third-grade wing of the elementary building. Moving three months after the school year started was not the daunting task it might have been if I hadn't lived through the weekend of emotional turmoil at the beginning of the year.

I haven't seen my friend in years, but we are both still teaching. I have her to thank for that. My goal is to pay it forward. When new teachers join the staff, I see the shaky smiles on their faces and remember the emotional and professional support my friend gave me.

–Stacy Vickers

My Return

What's going on? These lights are so bright! Why do they keep pushing on me? Where am I?

I thought I might be in handcuffs, but I'd done nothing wrong. *Lee should be the one arrested, not me.* I yanked on the strap around my right wrist first and then the left. With fingers pointed and my thumbs squeezed tight against my pinkies, I concentrated on slimming the profile of my hands as I wiggled and worked to be released. The lights went dim.

Someone pressed down hard on my shoulders. Big hands with hairy knuckles. He threatened, "Stop it!"

"Don't fight us," a calmer voice tried, but not convincing me.

Other people talked, but to each other and not to me. My mind was foggy. *Someone tell me what's going on!*

"Pam! Please stop." I recognized the voice of my sister, Deb, but my head was strapped in some kind of device, and I could only see what was immediately before me. "Calm down," she begged.

I fought.

The full weight of a body lay over my knees while straps tightened around my ankles. "Let them do what they need to do!" Deb yelled. She was angry, yet I was the one being accosted.

My lights went out.

I woke in a hospital room with my son and two daughters standing over me. Deb stood back, leaning against a wall. My wrists and ankles were no longer restrained, but my throat hurt and something had definitely made me weak and nauseous.

Deb did most of the explaining, and the kids filled in the blanks as my own memory returned me to the anger and events from earlier in the day.

I recalled that sweltering hot, July morning. Lee and I had been fighting for at least a week. He was an over-the-road truck driver and gone for many unaccountable hours. I knew he was cheating on me, and had been making myself crazy trying to prove it. I couldn't sleep. I couldn't eat. Thoughts of who, where, and why consumed me.

Initially, he denied the affair, but refused to offer evidence that he'd been faithful.

"I can forgive you, but I need to know the truth."

Lee remained silent, except to turn the guilt in my direction with indiscriminate threats and smiles of arrogant satisfaction.

"Just tell me and be done with it!"

Days of arguing and nights of unrest followed by days and nights of separation magnified our troubled relationship. As one of those people who feels the need to "fix" everything and never part or go to bed angry, dropping him off at his truck that morning and watching him walk away caused me anguish.

But the fighting continued over the phone. I would call. We would pick up the yelling where we left off, then one of us would hang up. I'd call again and the cycle would repeat. He must have heard a hundred offers to exchange a confession for my forgiveness and I a hundred long silences between his guilt shifting comments. We continued this phone battle for hours.

He eventually stopped answering my calls. That he cared so little about me and my affection infuriated me. I hadn't slept in more than three days. I was tired, body, mind and soul. Any emotion left inside me had been drained and left me empty.

Then I remembered seeing a dusty bottle of rum under the kitchen sink.

"Just a couple drinks, and I can sleep."

I'd never been much of a drinker, and I didn't care for the taste, but I anticipated the sleep that would give me at least a little peace.

Less than a year earlier, I'd had a back surgery, and now had leftover pain pills. I took one. The dangers of mixing the medication with alcohol were written, with bold lettering, on the bottle. I would have known better without reading the label, but I craved sleep and my mind wouldn't let me rest.

Just as my body relaxed and my eyelids had closed with sleep washing over me, Lee called. The fighting resumed.

After another hour of phone-fighting, I was no longer sleepy. My mind was re-wound and my blood stirring. I continued to drink the rum and scream intermittently into the phone. He yelled right back. It occurred to me that some innocent family, enjoying a pleasant road trip, was at risk because Lee was driving angry. I pictured gritting teeth, hands pounding on the steering wheel and his semi changing lanes erratically, but what could I do? By now, I was past the point of tipsy. I was pretty well intoxicated.

One more pill, and I can get some sleep. I washed it down with a gulp of rum, three-fourths of the bottle gone! I forced myself up from the kitchen chair and staggered into the bedroom, when somehow my alcohol-fogged brain reminded me it was past time to take my usual pills. Lee and I were still on the phone. I hung up on him while he was telling me how stupid and crazy I was, and how no other man would be with a woman like me. If he had found a better woman out there, he wouldn't take me up on my offer to let him go to her. My pills were chased by another shot of rum, and I added a couple more pain pills thinking (or not thinking) I hadn't taken any yet that day.

The bed felt so good, but I couldn't feel the pills taking their desired effect, other than having the room spin when I opened my eyes. While I waited for sleep, I picked up my phone and began punching numbers recalled from my mental phone book.

No one wanted to talk for long, and some of my best friends wouldn't even answer. My last thought before waking up briefly in the emergency room was that no one had time for me, and no one cared.

Deb and the kids were with me now, looking concerned, or was that agitation and frustration?

"It took a while to get help to you. We didn't know your address." My kids would have been able to find my house eventually, but I'd never given them an actual address. They were only mildly irritated by my phone calls and waiting for me to "sleep it off." What got their attention was a call I made to my brother, Greg. He'd been estranged from our family since Mom had died a couple decades earlier, but through my drunken tears, he recognized his sister's voice.

Even in the days before Mom died, it wasn't like me to call and just talk. Greg is seven years older than me and we'd never been close. He called Deb and told her, "Pam is messed up and there's nothing I can do." Sad, that he was so right. "Something must be really wrong for her to call me, and she's not making any sense."

Phone calls went back and forth while my sister, children, and a couple friends tried to find out where I lived. They knew the general area of town, but not the street or a close landmark.

"Brandie's the one who figured it out," Deb said. "She saved your life."

"How?"

Brandie answered matter-of-factly, not like a hero. "You told me Lee was a sex offender. His name and address is online."

I had to let that sink in. *I'm in a relationship with a sex offender.* Not anymore.

We lived on the south end of Peoria in a dangerous neighborhood. Everything stayed locked up tight, even when we were home. No one in the area would think of leaving windows or doors open or unlocked. It just wasn't smart or safe.

The fire department and EMTs came after the 911 call, and according to the EMT who talked to my sister, the door was locked. With the air running, all the windows were shut and locked. Before breaking down the door, one of the EMTs decided to check the backside of the house for a better, easier way to enter. The bedroom window was not only unlocked, it had no screen and was wide open.

They found me non-responsive. Not breathing and no heartbeat. Dead.

The almost empty bottle of rum and the pill bottle next to the bed told them there might still be some life in me worth saving. They say I got the paddles put to my chest and was shocked three or four times before and during the ambulance ride and two more times after I arrived in the emergency room.

My son, Brad, told me, "You almost didn't make it, Mom."

Hospitals are such humbling and humiliating places. Parts of my body that no one should see had been exposed. Evidence of my intoxication leached through my pores enough that everyone in the room must have noticed. Particles of waste that had been pumped from my stomach were somehow embedded in my hair. And that's only what people could see.

On the inside, I was still hurting. Every wrong relationship and terrible decision I'd ever made had brought me here. Lee had been the latest driver, but it was me who chose the path and set the course.

There is more to this story. Dave before Lee, Jerry before Dave, and Doug before Jerry … Men haven't treated me well. One of them slammed me around, fractured by back, messed up my hips and put me on disability for probably the rest of my life. Every one of them has broken a part of me. I was always the one to end the relationship, but each of them left me with less and feeling less than.

I'd say, "next time, I'll get it right. Next time, I'll be with a man who really loves me."

The doctors weren't sure about all the damage I'd done to my body as they reviewed my chart before I left the hospital. My chest had a massive bruise on the outside, and the deep ache from the shocks and CPR pained my every motion. My shoulders hurt from being restrained. Nothing they could do about that, except pain pills, which I was already taking because of my back and hips. My lab work came back almost normal, which alleviated everyone's fear of permanent liver damage. Doctors reminded me of how "lucky" I was and that my outcome would have been different if I had been a long-time, chronic drinker.

So I left the hospital with some bruising, a sore throat, an upset stomach, and a load of shame. A whole lot more of me was broken than what the doctors could see or I cared to talk about. Plus, I wondered if anyone would care enough to actually listen. Brad was afraid it would happen again and angry enough to walk away from me forever, but he didn't. He'd been my rock. Brandie, more reserved, sat quietly with her thoughts. I remember some of Bethany's behavior in the emergency room. She nearly had to be restrained as she told the doctors and nurses what needed to be done. It wasn't a good time for talking.

This is the place in my story where another miracle ought to happen. Right? I'd been found dead, or within minutes of death, and been revived because of a series of "coincidences." Yet, that wasn't enough. I needed more. You might be thinking, she needs God! And that would be the correct answer. But I was already a believer. God had already proven himself to me, and (at least on most Sundays) I trusted Him.

I wouldn't have considered myself a "church lady" back then, but I was. Keeping up appearances had kept me away from church and regular worship with His people, but nothing can separate me from God. I had fallen and I was broken, but I was God's. My heart and soul belonged to the Church (capital C). Other church ladies didn't know me, but I was their sister in Christ.

"Can anything ever separate us from Christ's love? Does it mean he no longer loves us if we have trouble or calamity, or are persecuted, or hungry, or destitute, or in danger, or threatened with death?" (Romans 8:35, NLT).

But what about the trouble and calamity we eagerly accept with our terrible choices? What if I'm hungry, destitute, in danger, and my life is threatened because I've made a series of stupid and selfish decisions?

"And I am convinced that nothing can ever separate us from God's love. Neither death nor life, neither angels nor demons, neither our fears for today nor our worries about tomorrow—not even the powers of hell can separate us from God's love. No power in the sky above or in the earth below—indeed, nothing in all creation will ever be able to separate us from the love of God that is revealed in Christ Jesus our Lord" (Romans 8:38-39, NLT).

Nothing I've done and nothing I can do will ever cause God not to love me. A decision I made years ago settled that I am His and He is mine. Now, my choice is whether I return to God on this side of Heaven or later.

First, I returned through music about Him—playing piano and singing words about how much Jesus loves me. Nothing had separated me from God's love. My return to a local church took a little while longer, a lot of courage, and multiple invitations from good friends.

–P. J. Hill

The Price of Caregiving

Two days before she passed away, it was just Shirley and me in her small apartment. Her son, Michael, needed a few things from the store and asked me to sit with her while he was gone.

Having attended the same church for many years, I'd seen her from a distance as we sat on opposite sides of the sanctuary and was amazed (or a bit intimidated) by her fierce independence. She lived through the pain of her cancer for three years, still doing her own housework, driving to the grocery store, and attending church most Sundays. Then her cancer spread. Her strength was gone. Michael and his brothers lived too far away to be daily caregivers. Our pastor became her first person to call.

When the hospice nurse who had visited her over the previous three years told our pastor it was no longer safe for her to live alone, he thought of me. I had worked as a volunteer caregiver, plus given my time to others with different sorts of needs and unusual circumstances before. He trusted me and instinctively knew Shirley and I would be a good fit.

The three of us agreed that I should be her core live-in caregiver and have others step in while I worked my regular day job. For the first four months, I slept on the daybed in her small office. During those last three months, Shirley needed a hospital bed and someone close by all the time. I moved into Shirley's room. Our beds were only inches apart. Nights were easier for both of us that way.

Michael had only been gone a little while when I peeked into the bedroom to check that Shirley was still breathing. I had worried for nothing. She opened her eyes as though sensing me in the doorway.

She put a scowl on her face and said "Go away. You're interrupting my talk with Jesus."

I understood and backed away. There are times when I wish people would leave me alone so I can have a conversation with Jesus, but I was saddened and felt awkwardly unnecessary after being so vital a part of her daily living. My ego was crushed.

I had a house, seven blocks from Shirley's apartment, but over the past seven months we had made a home together. Her strength and in-charge attitude brought out feelings of inadequacy in me at first. I worried about having nothing to offer her other than physical care, but she saw something in me; or maybe it's what she didn't see that made her want to pour every ounce of her accumulated wisdom into me—almost eighty years in total.

When I first moved in, she asked me to make supper. She observed as I maneuvered around her kitchen, not knowing what to expect from me, and having never raised a daughter, not knowing how to correct. She controlled her tongue, but expressed shock with a severely raised eyebrow at my clumsy handling of knives and timidity around her oven. I had no … almost zero experience in a kitchen.

If I had to guess what she was thinking, it would be, "Teach this girl how to cook!"

She sat at the small table in her kitchen, not hovering, just talking me through what I needed to do as I prepared our meals. She complimented me after every first bite, and I began to anticipate her approval.

One thing she loved to make (and eat) was chicken and wild rice soup. We made it together the first time, but soon she became more confident in my cooking abilities and would supervise my meal preparation from several feet away in her living room recliner. I liked having her close enough to observe, but also giving me space to exercise my confidence. The day came when I was on my own in the kitchen because Shirley was unable to get out of bed.

One afternoon she said "I want you to make some chicken and wild rice soup for me."

I started chopping and dumping ingredients, enjoying my new kitchen skills. Shirley's voice was in my head and talking me through every step. Once the pot was boiling, I took a picture and carried my phone to her for some well-deserved admiration. She smiled as she held my phone.

"Smells good."

Later came the true test. Tasting. She didn't want a big soup bowl as her appetite had steadily decreased. I placed a spoon and a child-sized serving of soup in front of her. She nodded. I needed her approval. It did look good, but I held my breath as she took that first bite. Her eyes closed and she sighed contentedly. Affirmation. Before she gobbled up the rest of the bowl, she asked for more. Both teacher and student had achieved success!

Shirley hadn't been sleeping through the night. She would wake, almost without fail, and have me turn her at 3:30 in the morning. That was when we would have our most intimate talks. We formed a treasured friendship in seven short months, at least from my perspective. We were two women, who at any other time in our lives, might never have shared a private fear or personal story. A kind of vulnerability had bonded client and caregiver. With Shirley and me, roles sometimes got reversed—not where it came to cooking, cleaning, or bathing and changing linens, but in caring about desires and things of the heart. A trust built between us.

I would miss our late night connections, but I didn't know it yet. Midnight snacks, 2:00 a.m. morphine doses, and starting a load of laundry before the sun came up was part of the deal. I knew enough about death and dying to understand that we can never say when, but since the day I made my first pot of chicken and wild rice soup, my assumption was that I would be there. Maybe even be holding her hand.

One morning I woke up tired before my feet even touched the floor. It was a much-needed day off from both of my jobs, and I would love to have been in my own bed, in my own home, and stay cozy for a while longer. Emotional upheaval, headaches and body aches had become my norm. I was stressed. I laid still for a few minutes, gearing up my mind to face another day.

The night before had been a restless one for both of us. I held my breath many times as I waited for Shirley to take her next one. When my phone rang, I tried putting a smile on my face but just didn't feel it. A friend from church asked about Shirley.

"Still breathing, six times a minute."

"I feel like I need to come sing for her. Would that be okay?"

"One of her sons will be here later this morning. If you could come before that?"

I met her at the door with a planted smile and tears, then directed her to the bedroom as though she needed to be told which way to turn in in the tiny place. All the while, I managed to put a smile on my face and fought tears. She sat on the bed to sing a few songs, and I returned to the living room. Her voice drifted easily and I listened to those timeless hymns knowing they'd been written especially for a day like Shirley and I were having. The singing only gave more tears permission to fall, and after a few songs, my friend gave me a hug and squeezed my hands before she stepped out the door with a promise to check in later.

Shirley's son showed up about an hour after that, but not before calling to ask what I'd like in the way of a Starbuck's breakfast. He looked refreshed since the last time I'd seen him, which was the morning after taking one of my night shifts for me.

"I don't know how you do that every night," he'd said.

I didn't tell him, but I hadn't slept a night through in almost seven months. I smiled and accepted his way of saying thank you.

Today was my day off and I had "me" stuff to do. When it came time to leave, I was torn. I didn't want to leave, yet I had plans. I had made sure she was clean, dry, comfortable and recently dosed with morphine before my relief caregiver or her son arrived. So terrified I'd been only a few months earlier to touch her or move her and potentially make her uncomfortable; and that day, I had moved, and rolled, and tugged and tucked like a pro.

The first time she said "I think I need some morphine," my anxiety hit the ceiling. I had been dreading the moment. The hospice nurse's instructions for drawing up the drug were clear and simple, yet I trembled. Physically, something fearfully potent was in my hands. Mentally, I was thinking back to when my grandfather was in the hospital fighting the pain of his cancer. They had given him morphine. It caused him to see things. I treasured the friendship Shirley and I had developed, and was afraid that morphine would alter her mind as well. A triple check of the right dosage and still unsure of myself, I silently prayed. Five minutes later, as the wrinkle in her forehead was gone and she was resting peacefully, I realized that morphine was just another word for relief.

By now, drawing up morphine into a syringe and measuring just the right dose had become second nature. I had done it "in the dark."

After a couple errands, I ended up at a friend's house for lunch and Bible study. We were almost done with our study when my phone rang. It was the other caregiver calling.

"She just died."

Hearing those words, although somewhat expected, seemed to take the air out of my lungs. I went back even though I wasn't scheduled for another hour and a half.

When I arrived, the apartment was full of people. The other caregiver, the on-call nurse, her hospice nurse who had been with her for the last three years, and the funeral director all spoke with reverent whispers. In the bedroom, her son was on one side of the hospital bed, and the pastor on the other, standing like guards over her.

I stepped in. Some tears and a hug from her son, then I was alone with her. A stuffed dog I had picked up on one of my day-off trips to a local park was next to her on the bed. With a little imagination I could have seen it crying too. I was holding that token of our friendship when one of the nurses came into the room to check on me. *Was I taking too long?* I think I was waiting for Shirley to open her eyes and ask for some soup or tell me to give her some alone time with Jesus.

Her son permitted me to stay another night in the apartment, seeing I needed more time to say goodbye. A friend brought me supper and another friend spent the evening talking and remembering with me. A third friend came later so I wouldn't spend the night alone.

For the last time, her son would call me in the morning and ask what I would like for breakfast. I was fine until he said, "See you in a little while, Kiddo."

Shirley and I were not family, and this wasn't the first time a client had died. But, as I grieved, and God provided comfort through friends, I was surprised by how much care this caregiver needed.

Random tears surprised me over the next week or so. They fell as I ordered purple roses (her favorite color) for the funeral. Tears were invited by something as ridiculous as a stuffed puppy dog, hugs at the funeral, and the dinner that followed. Several of us were not ready to say goodbye.

I missed our friendship, and honestly, I missed being needed. Grief, I've come to realize, is included in the price of caregiving. I'm still a caregiver, by profession and as a friend.

–Rebecca Price

About the Authors

Anita Allen loves golf and her son, Danny, but not usually in that order. Actually, Anita's life was slow in coming to any sort of order or follow any serious plan. For her, life almost didn't begin at all. Her early years were tough, but never boring. Anita has written many poems; most of them telling a story from her childhood or as a young adult. Many of them shed light on the pain she and her mother, Cora Lee, experienced. Talking to God with words that rhyme and a healthy sense of humor have saved her from several certain disasters, even during the eighteen years she gave to thousands of high school students and hundreds of teachers as their cafeteria manager! Friends might have called her "stubborn" in her former days, but as a church lady, we call what she has a steadfast faith. The book, *Porcelain Doll: A Church Lady Story* is based on Anita's life and poetry. It's due to be released in January of 2022.

Jenny Auxier grew up in Kansas City, Missouri and in church. Her husband, David, serves as a pastor in central Illinois, and they stay busy chasing their adorable three-year-old son, Andrew. Jenny currently teaches 6th grade, but has also taught in middle school and high school. She enjoys sewing, baking, and reading. It was during a week of Vacation Bible School that, with the total faith of a child, Jenny decided to follow Jesus. She was only six. Her favorite Bible verse is Ecclesiastes 3:11(ESV): "He has made everything beautiful in its time. He has also set eternity in the human heart; yet no one can fathom what God has done from beginning to end." As you read Jenny's stories, it's so clear how that seldom-quoted verse is special to her. She hopes you'll remember it, too.

Kristi West Breeden, a Christian publishing professional with 30 years of experience, is currently an associate editor for *Ideals*, an annual holiday book of art, poetry, and prose. Prior to that, Kristi worked for an author and singer to help distribute and create Christian-based books and music for children. During that time she had the opportunity to sing background vocals for children's music recordings. Kristi has been singing since she was old enough to hold a hymnal, and is part of her church's worship team. In her spare time, Kristi plays with her cat, Max, enjoys dreaming up new puns, and watches Cardinal's baseball and classic television shows with her husband, Neil. She also loves traveling the back roads and taking pictures of God's creation. Check out Kristi's blog, *The Maze of Our Lives*, to see what she's been pondering lately. Her favorite verse: "He comforts us in all our troubles so that we can comfort others. When they are troubled, we will be able to give them the same comfort God has given us" (2 Corinthians 1:4, NLT).

JoAnn Brown claimed a favorite Bible verse as a young girl: "For God so loved the world, that he gave his only begotten Son, that whosoever believeth in him should not perish, but have everlasting life" (John 3:16, KJV). Other verses have come to mean a lot to her, but those words sum up the gospel of Jesus Christ better than anything for JoAnn. She's been married to her husband, Bill, for 64 years. They have two daughters and four grandchildren. JoAnn and Bill loved boating and water skiing when their family was younger, "but now that we're older" she clarifies, "I'm happy to go to the library." JoAnn enjoys singing at church and teaching her ladies Bible class on Sunday mornings.

Dawn Cook has worked in public service for over twenty-five years. She is the current director of Tazewell County's Emergency Management Agency, an advisory board member of her community's Salvation Army, and past president of the Illinois Emergency Services Management Association. Dawn is married to George, has three children and three step-children. She enjoys traveling, planting flowers, watching TV and connecting with other women as an Independent Paparazzi Accessories Consultant. Family is both her priority and passion. She says her mother has always "given selflessly and been a rock to our family." Dawn strives to apply that same pattern when managing her own relationships. George and two of her children have Type 1 diabetes. Finding a cure would be a dream come true for their entire family. In the meantime, she trusts God's promise in Jeremiah 29:11 (NIV): "'For I know the plans I have for you,' declares the LORD, 'plans to prosper you and not to harm you, plans to give you hope and a future.'"

Holly Templeton Duckworth loves her entire family, but since having grandchildren, they make up the better part of her hobbies and interests. Whatever they are doing is what Holly wants to do or watch. She also enjoys being outdoors and gardening. Holly worked for twenty-two years as the site director of Southern Illinois University's Head Start program. Semi-retired, she is currently an office assistant for a Christian daycare. Her husband, Victor, has been a bivocational pastor for most of their forty years of marriage. She has held a variety of teaching, committee, and clerical positions in the churches where they've served. Together, they are coordinators of a Lay Renewal Ministry for the Illinois Baptist State Association. Holly says, "The things I have accomplished in this life are only because of Jesus." Her favorite verse is found in Philippians 4:13 (NIV): "I can do all things through Christ who strengthens me."

P. J. Hill is the mother of three, one son and a set of twin girls. She has six grandchildren, and takes an active role in raising two of her granddaughters. P. J. enjoys quilting, writing poetry, short stories, and songs. God gifted her with a talent for playing the piano. She shares that gift with her church family by serving on their praise team, and she sings, too! If the legacy she leaves for her children and grandchildren includes a love for music, that would make P. J. happy, but more importantly, she wants to point them to her Savior. Philippians 1:20–21 (KJV) is her favorite Bible verse: "According to my earnest expectation and my hope, that in nothing I shall be ashamed, but that with all boldness, as always, so now also Christ shall be magnified in my body, whether it be by life, or by death. For to me to live is Christ, and to die is gain." Ms. Hill considers the times God orchestrated circumstances in her life and repeats a common quote, "There but by the grace of God, go I." She prays her story will reach others who feel as lost as she once was, and that they find comfort and hope in the Savior who believes they are worth it!

Marilyn Hurt moved to Illinois from the big city of Indianapolis when she was a young woman and worked with children at a city mission for a while. If she *had* return to a job, that would be her choice. She is married to Chet and they have two adult children, Troy and Patty. Marilyn worked for a large retail chain store and then a popular fast-food restaurant before having three strokes that took her from the workforce. If Marilyn smiles when she says, "I'm gonna git you!" that means she likes you. Hers was one of the first smiles visitors would see as they entered her church's food pantry—"before COVID-19 changed everything." She can write faster than she speaks, and she doesn't mind doing dishes, laundry or making a bed. Marilyn loves to crochet. You won't hear her grumble unless you mention that, since COVID-19, she and Chet can't meet their friends for breakfast at McDonald's.

Ellene Lisanby (1931-2017) was a wife, mother, grandmother and "Granny" to her great-grandchildren. She wouldn't have wanted to list her many accomplishments in a bio such as this. Simplicity is the word she thought described her best. Ellene's greatest pleasure was found in serving other people. Her family came first, and after that she positioned herself in ministries and a career that served the needy and most vulnerable. She's remembered for her love of missions and for bringing good, clean fun to any event. Ellene's favorite verse: "Let not your heart be troubled; you believe in God, believe also in Me. In My Father's house are many mansions; if it were not so, I would have told you. I go to prepare a place for you. And if I go and prepare a place for you, I will come again and receive you to Myself; that where I am, there you may be also" (John 14:1–3, NKJV).

Judy Mandrell grew up on a small farm in mid-Illinois. Her summers were full of outdoor adventures with her pony, dog and cats. She still has a strong connection with and a love of nature. Judy is married to a wonderful Christian man. Their five children are grown, with children of their own. Two Pekingese pups fill their otherwise empty nest and require as much attention as toddlers. Her hobbies are writing, crocheting, and counted cross stitching. Giving family and friends presents made by her own hands brings her great joy. Judy's favorite Bible verse is: "Ask and it will be given to you; seek and you will find; knock and the door will be opened to you" (Matthew 7:7, NIV).

Cathy McAllister is a wife, mother, grandmother and great-grandmother. She enjoys reading mysteries and watching them on television with her husband, Joe. For twenty years she, and her best friend Joyce, had a successful craft business and loved traveling to shows and watching women admire their creations. Of course, they liked selling their crafts because that meant less packing for the trip home. Jesus Christ has been the most important person in her life since she was ten years old. He gave to her a passion for helping and serving people, but when asked about her favorite scripture, Cathy can't decide. "Every day, it's a different verse from the Bible that speaks to me. That's why it's called *The Living Word.*" Fun fact about Cathy: She always wanted to be a private investigator.

Robin McClallen has been actively volunteering in crisis pregnancy center ministries for nearly twenty years. She is passionate in her desire to see women supported in their choice to choose life and to find help and healing from past abortions. She and her husband of forty-four years have two amazing children and one extra-special grandchild. In her spare time she writes, kayaks, hikes, reads and endeavors to draw ever-closer to her gracious and loving Heavenly Father who saved her from *all* of her sins. She is the author of *"Free to Fly, A Novel of Post Abortion Healing"* available under her pen name, Savannah Grace Groden.

Stephanie Bridgeman-McClaskey is the youngest to contribute a story to this book. She still has a lot to learn, but is working hard at being a great mother to her son, Silas, and an honor student majoring in journalism. She loves writing and is passionate about using her words to renew hope for those still in dark places. "Pain has a purpose," she says. "Some come to Christ from a position of gratitude, but most of us found our way through despair." As a daughter to Gary and Cindy, Stephanie appreciates her family. Having been raised through the foster system, with thirteen siblings from different family dynamics, life has been complicated, but seldom boring, and always precious. Silas' father, Brendan, is a significant part of her life now and her biggest fan. They enjoy hiking, swimming, nature adventures, camping and cooking. When Stephanie looks back, she sees that God's heart and hands have protected her, even on the hardest days. "Keep your eyes up and feet moving forward. Don't put your faith in people or things. Keep your faith planted in Him!"

Jill McNicol loves teaching preschoolers on Sunday morning and playing piano for worship, but that is only where her service to the church begins. She is a past president of Illinois Women's Missionary Union and remains committed to mission service and missions education. Jill is single, with one young son who has four legs and goes by the name Finnegan. She enjoys reading, coloring and speaking to women's groups. She is the Administrator for the Marion (IL) County Department of Human Services, having devoted twenty-six years to her community. Given the stories provided by preschoolers and her day job, Jill "threatens" to write a book and knows it would be a best-seller. Parents, and even some clients (nameless, of course) would rush to buy up every copy to protect their innocence or guilt, whichever the case may be! Jill laughs a lot, but she would also want you know that when life is tough, or she lacks confidence and courage, she finds comfort and hope in God's Word. Psalm 121 is her favorite.

Aletha Oakley loves her family, the church and music. She and her husband, F.M., came from Tennessee to Illinois in the 1950s. Both of them educators, F.M. gave the better part of his life to teaching high school biology and being faithful to God as a deacon in their church. Aletha taught English for a while, but has spent the majority of her life (and years) devoted to raising a family and serving her church as music/choir director. Her life reflects the message of her favorite Bible verse: "Trust in the LORD with all thine heart; and lean not unto thine own understanding. In all thy ways acknowledge him, and he shall direct thy paths" (Proverbs 3:5–6, KJV).

Jan O'Bleness, her friends would say, is "a gal who will go the extra mile." That extra mile is on the golf course when the weather allows. Sometimes it's with her husband, Jerry, and a bunch of other Corvette owners raising money for St. Jude. Having no children of her own, she's always gone the extra mile for her nieces, nephews and grand-nieces and nephews. Jan enjoys watching the many furry creatures who visit her back yard, but her favorite four-legged creatures are two long-haired dachshunds named Oakley and Kacie. Jan's most loved Bible verse is "For by grace are ye saved through faith; and that not of yourselves: it is the gift of God: Not of works, lest any man should boast" (Ephesians 2:8–9, KJV).

Diana Parson is a "word teacher." After forty-six years of instructing writing, composition, literature, speech, drama, and journalism from preschool to university level, she still writes, edits and tutors. She and her husband of forty-five years have one son and three grandchildren. They love to travel, read, and enjoy both creating and observing art. They also have a passion for small group teaching within the church. Philippians 4:8 (NIV) is her guide verse for judging life priorities: "Finally, brothers and sisters, whatever is true, whatever is noble, whatever is right, whatever is pure, whatever is lovely, whatever is admirable —if anything is excellent or praiseworthy—think about such things." Her blog, "Right Here, Right Now, Glory Be" is viewable at: www.glorybug.wordpress.com.

Rebecca Price is the activity director at an assisted living facility. She spends much of her "off" time with the elderly, helping families to fill the gaps between community services and real need. Rebecca says, "The elderly should feel loved and appreciated." When she's not working or volunteering, Rebecca enjoys reading, writing and scrapbooking. The goal of her current writing project, *Dadventures*, is to minister to others by drawing them closer in relationship to their Heavenly Father. Her favorite verse is: "I can do all things through Christ who strengthens me" (Philippians 4:13, NKJV).

Natalie Schnoor enjoys going down a road she's never been on before just to see where it goes. She also likes reading Christian mysteries and watching Hallmark murder mysteries. Natalie loves surprises, which is why she goes fishing and treasures the days she gets to hang out with one, or all seven, of her grandkids. She and her husband of thirty-five years have two sons and two daughters plus lots of young people who've been adopted into their family. She loves them all! Making one brave decision changed everything for her favorite woman in the Bible (Esther) and for Natalie as well. The extraordinary way God has shown His love to her and her family has purposed her heart for sharing His love. That's why she teaches in the children's department at her church. Kids love surprises and aren't afraid to let it show. Natalie wants her story to tell women, children and even men, "You can never be in too deep or go so far that God can't surprise you."

Kathy Stanford is passionate about God, her family, Bible study and prayer. Married to an Army veteran, she and her husband have two married sons and six grandsons. She has traveled to eleven countries and many of the United States, but finds herself staying closer to home these days. She currently spends her free time reading, watching light movies and learning to quilt. Kathy is active in women's ministry and leads a Bible study at her church. She has taught younger preschoolers for eleven years. One of her favorite verses is John 14:6 (NLT): "Jesus told him, 'I am the way, the truth, and the life. No one can come to the Father except through me.'" Another verse she loves is Isaiah 43:2 (NLT): "When you go through deep waters, I will be with you. When you go through rivers of difficulty, you will not drown. When you walk through the fire of oppression, you will not be burned up; the flames will not consume you."

Dalene Stewart tells people who question the pronunciation of her German name, "Just remember you will have a better *day* if you *lean* on the Lord. Just say *Daylean*!" The fairly recent loss of her husband taught her that what needs to be done next is often hard to figure out. She struggled with making the simplest decisions in the months that followed her crisis of grief, but since being widowed, she is learning to "lean." She hasn't lost her love of reading, quilting, taking short walks, cooking or spending time with family. All those things help to pass time and keep her busy. When that's not enough she prays about and works on plans to serve God in the area of grief support. Dalene's favorite verse provides comfort and holds the answer: "Trust GOD from the bottom of your heart; don't try to figure out everything on your own. Listen for GOD's voice in everything you do, everywhere you go; he's the one who will keep you on track. Don't assume that you know it all" (Proverbs 3:5-6, MSG).

Sandra Taylor enjoys watching movies, sewing, knitting, needlework and quilting. She has worked as a Tupperware lady, been a volunteer for the M.A.D.D. organization, holding both local and statewide offices, plus served in various church positions at three churches throughout her life. Leading a quilting group that makes lap quilts for cancer patients is a perfect way for Sandra to combine pleasure with her desire to encourage and serve others. She and her husband, Larry, have three children, four grandchildren and two great-grandchildren. Sandra's pet peeve is when people misuse or misquote her favorite verse of Scripture and say, "God won't give us more than we can handle." Read *all* of 1 Corinthians 10:13 (NIV): "No temptation has overtaken you except what is common to mankind. And God is faithful; he will not let you be tempted beyond what you can bear. But when you are tempted, he will also provide a way out so that you can endure it."

Stacy Vickers is a veteran teacher of twenty-seven years. She believes wholeheartedly that God has called her to serve in the mission field of a public school. It is a place she can reach children, parents, and coworkers each day even if she cannot preach His Name directly. Her family is second in her life only to her Heavenly Father. She loves her local church and sings with their praise band, Spirit and Truth. Stacy is grateful for the God who drew her in as a child and holds her close through the good and the bad. Her life verse has sustained her through divorce, the loss of both her parents, and currently…teaching virtually. "What then shall we say in response to these things? If God is for us, who can be against us?" (Romans 8:31, NIV).

Susan Walker worked for twenty years in the field of social work before making a move to the private university setting. She has been a staff member in the counseling and student support departments of two different universities over the last seventeen years. Susan is married to T. J., has one daughter, a son-in-law and two grandchildren. Her hobbies include reading (everything!), studying the Bible, apologetics, mowing the three acres that surround their home, seeing her grandbabies when she can, and trying to get words on blank pages. Saved at the age of ten, Susan describes her life with Christ as moments and seasons of walking and growing, falling and getting back up, sinning and being forgiven, but always being brought back to a place of thankfulness and loving the Lord. Her greatest concern is for people who don't know Jesus, and she is passionate about praying for others. She is reminded daily of 2 Corinthians 5:7 and her need to "walk by faith, and not by sight." Another of her favorite verses is "to open their eyes so that they may turn from darkness to light, and from the power of Satan to God, that they may receive forgiveness of sins and an inheritance among those who have been sanctified by faith in Me" (Acts 26:18, NASB).

Lindsay Wineinger, along with her husband Nathan and three girls, lives in Princeville, Illinois where they own and operate the local feed store as well as help maintain their family cattle operation. When she's not taking care of her family, her chickens, or the cows, you can find Lindsay goofing around on her Instagram account @theWineingerFarms or traveling who knows where. God willing, by the time you are reading this, the Wineinger Restaurant, the Feed Store, will be open for business. God is good. God is in control. "I would have lost heart, unless I had believed that I would see the goodness of the LORD in the land of the living" (Psalm 27:13, NKJV).

Dawn Wright is blessed to be mom to four boys and a daughter. She and her husband of fifteen years were former high school sweethearts when God brought them together for a "yours, mine, and ours" family. Dawn adores kids of all ages, but especially the pre-K's and kindergarteners she teaches on Sunday mornings and the teen Girls of Grace who ask hard questions and keep her looking to her Bible for answers. She is co-director for WinGs (Women in God's Service) where women of all stages of Christian discipleship are welcomed and nurtured. Remembering what 2 Timothy 3:16 (NKJV) says keeps her motivated to prepare lessons for all ages (children who are barely potty-trained, teens, and adult women). "All Scripture *is* given by inspiration of God, and *is* profitable for doctrine, for reproof, for correction, for instruction in righteousness." Because she has been there, Dawn's heart breaks for those stuck in human trafficking, who struggle with addiction, and children who are abused, neglected, or on the streets. She applies her life verse to every aspect of daily living: "For God has not given us a spirit of fear, but of power and of love and of a sound mind" (2 Timothy 1:7, NKJV). In her spare time, Dawn is a cosmetologist and cleans the building where she attends church.

Rita Klundt had an unrelenting idea: Getting women who love Jesus and His church together and having them tell a personal story might open doors of opportunity for sharing the truth about who Jesus really is and dispel some of the myths about "church ladies." She was still employed as a nurse when all this started, but already working on her second career as an author, speaker and story collector. A few friends caught her vision and couldn't refuse her invitation to swap a short story. *Real Life. Real Ladies: Short Stories from the Pew* was born. One of Rita's favorite Bible verses is, "Delight yourself in the LORD, and he will give you the desires of your heart" (Psalm 37:4, ESV). This book became more real as each personal and true story was added to the manuscript. Now, it is the desire of her heart to have other women read these stories and for conversations that include Jesus to begin. Rita prays that the Lord will find delight in what she and twenty-six other women have accomplished. If you'd like to know more about Rita, check out her memoir. *Goliath's Mountain* is a passionate, poignant and tragic love story that gives you a view into the heart of a family touched by mental illness and suicide. It won't leave you hopeless. Follow Rita and watch for more great stories at www.ritaklundt.com.

Made in the USA
Monee, IL
27 May 2021

68709124R00105